The Republic of Uruguay, South America

Its Geography, History, Rural Industries, Commerce, and General Statistics; With Maps

By Uruguay Consulado, London

Published by Pantianos Classics

ISBN-13: 978-1-78987-316-0

First published in 1883

Contents

Preface to the First Edition .... *iv*
Preface to the Second Edition .... *v*

The Republic of Uruguay, South America 6

General Description 6

The Capital 16

The Rural Districts 20

General Statistics 46

Trade and Commerce 60

Public Revenue 67

Public Works and Institutions 77

Money, Weights and Measures 82

Preface to the First Edition

DURING the last twenty years, more than a score of works by various English authors have been written on the resources, physical characteristics, government, history, and social Condition of the countries bordering on the River Plate.

The two Platine States are the Argentine Republic and the Republic of Uruguay, But the so-called River Plate is little more than the estuary of its two great affluents — the River Paraná and the River Uruguay.

Many hundreds of miles from its confluence with the Plate, the Paraná forms the southern and eastern boundaries of the Republic of Paraguay, which is again bounded on the west by the River Paraguay, a branch of the Paraná. The River Paraguay in its passage southwards touches the confines of Bolivia, and both rivers have their respective sources in the Sierras in the interior of Brazil.

The Uruguay also rises in a province of Brazil, and after a course of 1020 miles falls into the River Plate, within a short distance of the mouth or delta of the Parand.

The tract of the continent of South America watered by these great rivers and their branches is enormous. A portion of the Empire of Brazil and of the Argentine Republic, the Republic of Paraguay, and the Republic of Uruguay, are commercially connected by sea, and by the river communication due to the River Plate and its tributaries.

In the works referred to on the countries of the Plate, the Republic of Uruguay has, generally speaking, been alluded to incidentally. In one of the latest, however, the 'Handbook of the River Plate Republics,' [1] an interesting and detailed account will be found of the . capital and rural departments of Uruguay.

In the present pamphlet nothing is attempted beyond a general description of the Republic of Uruguay, and an endeavour to embody, in a readable form, the recent and official statistics of the country.

In regard to emigration, it may be stated that whilst the Government of the Republic of Uruguay has made efficient provision for the reception and assistance of emigrants, it has, hitherto, made no effort to influence anything in the shape of emigration propaganda.

The statistics it publishes are comprehensive and accurate. The general reader, or intending emigrant, can, from their perusal, form his own conclusions. The Government Statistical Department at Montevideo, which has latterly been under the direction of M. Adolphe Vaillant, [2] is a credit to the Republic and an example to older countries.

London, January, 1881.

[1] By M. G. and E. T. Mullhall. Edward Stanford, Charing Cross, London. 1875. Out of print, but a Spanish edition is still obtainable.
[2] Since this was written the Republic has had to deplore the loss of M. Yaillant. He died in 1881. He has been succeeded in the Statistical Department by Don Federico Nin Reyes.

Preface to the Second Edition

There still seem many who are anxious to possess statistical information in a small compass in regard to the Republic of Uruguay. The first edition of the present pamphlet, published in 1881 for gratuitous distribution, is long since exhausted.

It has been thought advisable to reprint the compilation in a more complete form, with a new map, and fuller details in respect to the sheep and cattle industries, and other subjects of immediate interest; and to offer the work for public sale in the usual way. For this purpose the publisher has taken at his own risk the MS. prepared at the expense and under the supervision of the Consul-General of Uruguay in London, who is interested solely in disseminating in this country an accurate knowledge of the Republic.

The new official statistics quoted are those of 1881 and the beginning of 1882. They are for the most part taken from the Report of the Minister of Finance, presented to the Legislature of the Republic in 1882; and also from the Report of the Statistical Department for the same year.

Much assistance has been gained from the 'Album of the Oriental Republic of the Uruguay,' prepared for presentation during the Continental Exhibition at Buenos Aires, by the Authors of the 'Album' Messrs. F. A. Berra, Agustin de Vedia, and Carlos M. de Pena.

Mr. Ph. H. Rathbone, Chairman of the Prange Estancia Company, Liverpool, has kindly given permission to print the extracts which will be found in the following pages from that gentleman's recent and valuable 'Report of a Visit to the Sheep and Cattle Farms of the Banda Oriental.'

London, 1883.

The Republic of Uruguay, South America

General Description

The Republic of Uruguay is officially known as the Oriental Republic of the Uruguay, and familiarly called the *Banda Oriental,* from its geographical position on the eastern side or left bank of the large river from which it takes its name.

The territory of the Republic is comprised between the 30th and 35th degrees of latitude S., and 53° 25' 5" and 57° 42' 25" of longitude W. It is irregular in form, and in some sense a peninsula; having a seaboard to the eastward on the Atlantic of 200 miles; a coast-line on the south and south-west on the estuary of the Plate of 155 miles; and a shoreline to the westward along the River Uruguay of 155 miles. Its northern boundaries, separating the Republic from Rio Grande do Sul, a province of the Brazilian Empire, are Lake Merim, the secondary rivers, the Chuy, the Yaguaron, and the Cuareim, and a *cuchilla,* or ridge of hills, known by the name of Santa Ana.

In regard to extent of territory as well as number of inhabitants, the Republic of Uruguay ranks low in the scale amongst the countries of the New World. Its area is not over 7,036 square leagues, and by the highest estimate its population cannot much exceed 450,000. But in some important respects it assumes a very enviable position compared with other States, either of South America or of Central America.

Independently of its temperate climate and physical characteristics, resembling those of the most favoured European countries, it is absolutely free from any vestige of that indigenous, or Indian population, which, in many South American countries, is still the chief social and political bane. Even the Africans imported in former years as slaves, and who, until lately, formed the mass of the soldiery of the Republic, and were largely employed as household servants and in other menial capacities, have now nearly disappeared. The Creole population itself in the whole of the Republic is scarcely more than two to one compared with the foreigners; whilst in. the metropolitan department of Montevideo, the native population of Spanish extraction, and of mixed Indian and European blood, exceeds by very little the number of residents of other nationalities. [1]

The proportions are 590 natives, 400 foreigners, and ten Africans in every 1000 inhabitants. By Article viii. of the Constitution, the sons of foreigners born in the country are treated as citizens of the Republic, and, it must be borne in mind, are included as natives in the foregoing estimates.

It is a fact, perhaps unexampled in any other country, that in the department of Montevideo there are 5372 foreigners who possess land and houses as freehold property, whilst there are only 2904 native freeholders. The foreign population of that department consists principally of Spaniards, Italians, and French. The Spaniards and French are mostly from the Basque provinces of their respective countries.

Estimated by the amount of her exports and imports, the relative position of Uruguay can be appreciated at once, by taking the comparatively large states of Latin America, the Empire of Brazil, the Argentine Republic, Chile, Peru, and Mexico, in the order of their commercial importance, and placing the Republic of Uruguay next, or sixth in the list; where according to trade statistics, she duly appears.

In National Schools for primary and gratuitous education, the Banda Oriental compares favourably, not only with South American countries, but with most countries in the world. In the United States of North America, the number of school children in proportion to the population is over 10 per cent.; in Canada it is 6 per cent.; in the Argentine Republic, 4 per cent.; in Chile, 4 per cent. In Uruguay, it was calculated that there were in 1879, 19,573 scholars at the National Schools, or 4½ per cent, in proportion to the population. This, of course, is irrespective of private schools, where the number of pupils is, more or less, 13,000.

According to the latest statistics (1882), it is said that 40,000 children of both sexes receive the benefits of public instruction; that is, one in seventeen of the population, or nearly 6 per cent.; still, it has been estimated that there are over 100,000 children from 5 to 15 years of age in the Republic.

In the Empire of Brazil the proportion is not 1 per cent.; and for Mexico, Peru, and other Spanish American countries no educational statistics are at hand, and in some cases they probably do not exist.

In comparing the social and commercial position of Uruguay with that of other countries of the New World, it is well to notice that amongst the 16 states of Latin origin, there is Brazil with a population of ten millions, and an area of 3,100,104 square miles; Mexico with a population of over nine millions, and an area of 1,030,442 square miles; the Argentine Republic with a population over two millions, and an area of 1,290,000 square miles. Then follow such states as Peru, Chile, Venezuela, Columbia, with populations varying from one to three millions, and with areas varying from 131,000 to 473,000 square miles. Among the smaller states with populations varying from 80,000 to 450,000, and with areas varying from 9500 to 80,000 square miles, Uruguay stands first in regard to population, and is second only to Paraguay in extent of territory. The respective areas of the two countries are 76,000 and 80,000 square miles. Either of the two is considerably larger than England and Wales.

It is evident that the importance of a country is not to be estimated either by the absolute number of its population, or by the extent of its territory. In the higher respects of advancement in commerce and civilisation, as well as in the superior character of the population as a question of race — forming so valuable a guarantee for the future — the Republic of Uruguay stands amongst the first of the American States of Spanish origin.

Her wonderful advance within the last quarter of a century may be due mainly to her geographical position; but it can also fairly be ascribed to the complete religious tolerance, as well as to the general liberality of the government of the Republic; to the social freedom and equality which exists within the different classes of society; to the energy and business capacities of the native population; and, above all, to their exceeding hospitality to foreigners.

In a very general sense, the history of the Banda Oriental may be said to date from the beginning of the sixteenth century, when the Rio de la Plata was first discovered by Juan Diaz de Solis. But in point of fact, the territory between the River Uruguay and the Atlantic, and to the south of the present frontier of Brazil, was, for more than a century after that period, all but abandoned to the savage tribes of unknown origin, who inhabited the banks of the great rivers in those regions. [2] The country remained little more than a pasture-ground for herds of wild cattle and horses, which the Spaniards, who had introduced them from Europe, left to multiply unheeded. The first settlers seem to have preferred the opposite shore of the River Plate, and the borders of the rivers Parana and Paraguay. The objects ever present to their minds, were the gold and treasures of the earth they imagined might exist further towards the interior of the new land. It was not until the seventeenth century, that the wild herds of cattle in the Banda Oriental attracted the notice of the Portuguese, who had partially peopled the coasts of the territory now known as Brazil. The Portuguese freely carried off the cattle, on the pretext that the country on the left bank of the River Uruguay to the shores of the Rio de la Plata belonged to the crown of Portugal. The Spaniards asserted a preferent claim, on the plea of their having founded, in 1624, the town of Santo Domingo Soriano. The principal settlement of the Portuguese was at Colonia del Sacramento, on the eastern shore of the River Plate, immediately in front of Buenos Aires. It was founded in 1680, and is still known as Colonia, a half-deserted little port, with vestiges yet visible of the old Portuguese fortifications. Although distant thirty miles from Buenos Aires, it is often seen from that city, in the calm weather preceding a storm, as a mirage high above the horizon.

The founding of the town and fort of Colonia del Sacramento, by the Portuguese, was the event that first led to a series of long struggles for the possession of the Banda Oriental. For a century and a quarter, the country belonged nominally and alternately to the Spaniards and Portuguese. . The real history of Uruguay can scarcely be said to have commenced until the beginning of the present century; and its history as an independent state dates only from the year 1828.

Early in the nineteenth century, the question of dominion was finally settled in favour of the Spaniards; and in the meantime, in spite of wars, the Banda Oriental was being peopled, and civilization continued to advance. In the central districts, as well as on the coasts of the Atlantic and of the large rivers, the Spaniards had founded many small towns and ports, the most important of which was Montevideo.

In the year 1726, the Captain-General, Don Bruno Mauricio de Zabala, officially established the limits of that city and of the adjoining territory. The boundaries of the latter were, independently of the River Plate, the range of mountains near Maldonado on the north east; the rivers Cebollaté and Yi to the north and west; and the river Santa Lucia in the south and west. The area comprised within these limits was at that time thought sufficient, not only for the settlers, who then numbered about 300 families, but for their remote descendants. The productions of the soil according to an official report made in 1787 were, in addition to a natural and luxuriant pasturage, wheat, barley, flax and small quantities of hemp. [3] Farms existed high up in the mountainous district of Minas, on the banks of the small and rapid streams, the Metal, San Francisco and Campanero, which the settlers utilized for the purposes of irrigation. At the sides of the rivers trees grew abundantly, and served for firewood and the building of huts, but not for general building purposes, as the fibre of the native wood was not close and firm enough for timber. Bread and beef were then the common aliment of the settlers, who generally farmed their own lands. About one-third laboured for other proprietors. So near to Montevideo as the San José and the Santa Lucia, grains of gold were found in the beds of the streams flowing into those rivers; but at that era there was neither the necessary skill nor machinery to profitably wash the auriferous sand and gravel. The old document, here quoted, quaintly adds, that in the district called Las Minas, lead, silver, copper, and gold, existed; but so mixed or bound together, that those who tried to separate them "lost their time and their money." Even in those days it was discovered that in that country the most advantageous objects of industry were hides and tallow. The process of salting hides had just commenced; and it was hoped that with experience, the art would eventually arrive at perfection. Great expectations were raised in regard to wheat, if only a system of barter, for cotton, timber and mate could be established, by land and water conveyance, with the Jesuit Missions of Paraguay. Already the necessity was foreseen of domesticating the cattle, instead of allowing them to run wild, and by their wanderings occasion disputes amongst neighbouring landowners.

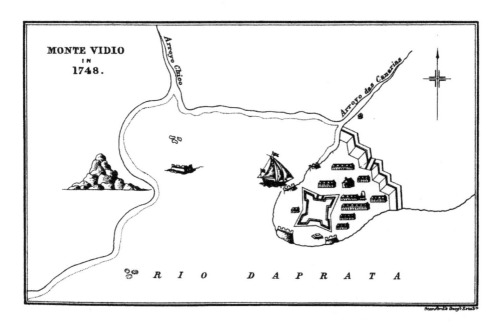

In the early days of the Spanish settlements in these regions, the whole of the River Plate district was included in the Viceroyalty of Peru. Subsequently a separate vice-royalty was created in Buenos Aires; and the Banda Oriental, which had been subject to the Colonial Government of Paraguay, Vas transferred to that of Buenos Aires. At the beginning of the century, Montevideo was ruled by a military and political governor appointed by the Crown of Spain. Maldonado, Colonia, and other places were subject to special military commands. The population of the capital was at that time about 15,000; and the same number of people existed in the interior of the province. Colonia had made rapid advance under the dominion of the Portuguese, and was the seat of an active commerce with Europe and the neighbouring Spanish settlements; but the last time it was taken by the Spaniards, the town was destroyed; and it gradually sank into its present insignificance. Maldonado, though situated on the Atlantic coast, and being the port nearest to the mining districts and to the largest cattle-growing departments, and possessing a natural harbour of some extent, has never made any considerable progress. The place is noted, however, as having possessed the first *Saladero* of any importance established in the country. Montevideo, in 1730, six years after its official creation, was a strong place from a military point of view, and its streets were planned out and named. The city contained a hospital, schools, and a theatre. The foundations were already laid of the Cathedral, which has only recently been completed. At the beginning of this century Montevideo was a prosperous commercial port, and numbered amongst its inhabitants a few English merchants. It was in such a position when an event happened which led indirectly to others that have proved of serious importance in the recent history of Uruguay. The commander of an English expedition, on its way to the Cape of Good Hope, conceived the idea of taking possession of Buenos Aires, the capital of the Spanish viceroyalty. This design was accordingly effected in June 1806; but in the month of August in the same year the invaders were expelled. In the following year the English returned with a considerable force under General Whitelock. On February 3, 1807, as a preparatory operation, they took Montevideo by storm; and afterwards occupied Colonia, Las Piedras, Canelones and San José, which they held until September 9th; when by the terms of a capitulation more disgraceful even than his defeat by the Spanish troops and citizens of Buenos Aires on his attempting to enter that city — Montevideo and the other places held by the British troops in the Banda Oriental were formally surrendered by General Whitelock.

The militia of the Banda Oriental had been organised and drilled after the first invasion, for it was expected that the English would return; and the troops of the Banda Oriental, under the command of General Liniers, subsequently took an active part in the defence of Buenos Aires. After the defeat of the British, it was Liniers who insisted that the surrender of Montevideo and other places held by the invaders in the Banda Oriental should be included in the terms of capitulation.

Hitherto, in the Spanish colonies on the borders of the River Plate, as in other parts of South America, the Creole population were held in little esteem by the Spaniards, who monopolised all offices of importance, and denied to those born in the country, common political privileges, and treated them as an inferior race. The part which the natives of Buenos Aires, and of the Banda Oriental, had taken in repelling the British attack, and the pusillanimous conduct displayed by the Spanish commander at Montevideo, had inspired the people with a high notion of their own invincibility, and a proportionate contempt for the regular troops of the King of Spain. The authority of the existing viceroy soon gave place to that of General Don Santiago Liniers, who was named viceroy in his stead. The Governor of Montevideo, as well as the Cabildo, pronounced against Liniers at the end of 1808, and in January 1809 the Spanish or royal troops in Buenos Aires revolted against the assumption of power by the "patriots" or native forces. In that city the royal troops and authorities were vanquished, and the patriot revolution triumphed completely on the 25th May, 1810. The Junta, or government there established, endeavoured to gain the adhesion of all the authorities and of the people in the viceroyalty. But the Spaniards still in power in Montevideo refused their adhesion, and declared war against the revolutionary Government in Buenos Aires. The Junta in the latter city then sowed the seeds of revolt in the Banda Oriental, and sent troops to support the patriots, confiding the command of the Uruguay militia to Don Jose Artigas. After various encounters, and the rising in mass of the rural population of the Banda Oriental, the power of Spain in the Rio de la Plata was subdued for ever, by the taking of Montevideo in June 1814, by the Buenos Airean general, Alvear.

It was then that the succession of *caudillos,* or military chieftains, which has proved the bane of these young republics, commenced. It has continued up to a very recent date, but latterly, and for many years past, with diminished force, until the era of pronunciamientos may now be said to have died out.

After the triumph of the revolution, the Banda Oriental was formed into a separate province, with the same privileges enjoyed by others in the Argentine Confederation. General Artigas had acquiesced in that arrangement, but claimed for himself the post of Governor of Montevideo. This was not acceded to by the authorities at Buenos Aires. In February 1815, he obliged the government of Montevideo to withdraw their troops from the city; and carrying the war into the Argentine provinces he established a military despotism and an anarchy remembered to this day with horror.

About the same time the troops, and the most distinguished generals of Buenos Aires, were engaged in assisting in the War of Independence then raging on the distant slopes of the Andes, east and west The Brazilian Government fearing that the anarchy occasioned by Artigas might extend to its own territory, and calculating that the Argentine Government was unable to expel him, thought the opportunity favourable for the occupation of the Banda Oriental by Portuguese and Brazilian forces. Accordingly troops were sent from Lisbon; and under the command of General Lecor, the Brazilian militia and Portuguese troops, on the pretence of restoring order, invaded the province at three distinct points; and on the 20th of January, 1817, they entered the city of Montevideo.

The government of Buenos Aires at first seemed to countenance the invasion; but afterwards, seeing that Brazil intended conquest, it was inclined to support Artigas on certain conditions, which the *Caudillo* did not think fit to accept. Single handed, with the undisciplined militia of Uruguay and the provinces of Santa-fé, Entre-rios, Corrientes and the Missions he had overrun, he gallantly fought against the Portuguese and Brazilians for three years; but continually defeated, he was ultimately obliged to take refuge in Paraguay, where he was persecuted by another *Caudillo,* Ramirez of Entre-rios.

The administration of the Portuguese general, Lecor, in Montevideo, was in the highest degree exemplary and liberal. Private interests were respected; and public institutions preserved and fomented. Captivated by his politic government, the conservative classes in the city were easily prevailed upon to favour the ambition of Portugal; and in a congress of Orientals convened in July 1821 by General Lecor, it was decreed that the Banda Oriental should be incorporated in the United Kingdom of Portugal, Brazil and Algarbes, under the title of the *Cisplatine State.*

Subsequently, when Brazil declared her independence of the crown of Portugal, it became a question whether the Cisplatine State should belong to Portugal or to Brazil, or return to her allegiance to the Argentine Confederation, then called the United Provinces of La Plata.

In the Banda Oriental itself, there were various political parties who sided with one or other of these propositions; but owing to the skill of Brigadier Souza de Macedo, it was ultimately decided, without much bloodshed, that the people should take the oath of allegiance to the newly-created Empire of Brazil.

About the end of 1823, and the beginning of 1824, the unhappy little state took once again a fresh appellation — *Cisplatina* — and duly became part of the dominions of Dom Pedro, first Emperor of Brazil.

The province of Buenos Aires during these events had become isolated from the United Provinces, and was not strong enough to enforce by arms a protest she had made against the military occupation of the Banda Oriental by Brazil. She, however, watched her opportunity. Republican refugees from Uruguay had been perpetually agitating in Buenos Aires for the recovery of the Banda Oriental from the power of the new Empire. A few of them, to the number of *thirty-three* — a number henceforth of historic fame — conspired together, and undertook to brave the chances of invading the Cisplatine provinces. On the memorable day, April 19th, 1825, they put foot on their native soil, under the command of Juan Antonio Lavalleja. This small party of invaders carried with them some saddles, with horse-gear, a few pistols and old muskets, and sufficient money to pay ordinary expenses.

The audacity — the bravery of the immortal *thirty-three,* was much favoured by the sparse population of the country, and by the ease with which irregular cavalry could be maintained and recruited unobserved, in wild and undulating pasture lands, abounding in food for man and horse. To these facilities, indeed, can be ascribed the success of many paltry revolutions which have occurred in the countries bordering on the River Plate, from that time until within a very recent period,, when the face of the country has undergone changes due to advancing civilisation.

The invaders had to encounter, not only the Brazilian troops, posted at certain points, but also the hostility, perhaps to them more formidable; of the *Caudillo* Rivera, who had succeeded Artigas, and had allied himself to the Brazilians. In ten days, however, Rivera was captured; and obliged to place his cavalry and what forces he possessed under the orders of the *thirty-three*. With these forces and other recruits, the invaders were soon in a position to besiege Montevideo; and in two months from the day of their landing they established a revolutionary government at Florida. Within four months, the assembly of the people's representatives annulled the incorporation of the state with Brazil, and united it to the rest of the River Plate provinces. In the fifth month, Rivera gained a brilliant action at the Rincon de Haedo. In the sixth month, the Orientals won the famous victory on the plains of Sarandi; and on the 24th of October, 1825, the Argentine Congress ratified the re-incorporation of the Banda Oriental with the United Provinces of La Plata.

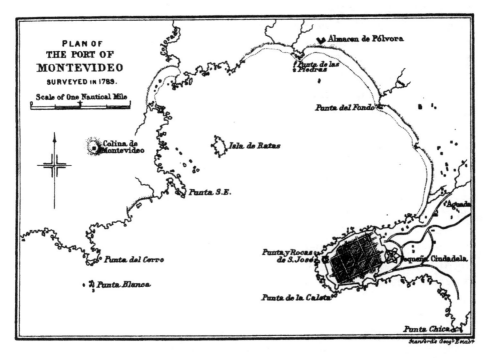

As a natural consequence, the Emperor of Brazil the following year declared war against the Argentine Republic. The Argentine General, Alvear, subsequently invaded the territory of Brazil; his vanguard consisting of Orientals under Lavalleja. The Buenos Aireans had in the interval armed a naval squadron, which was placed under the command of an Irishman, Admiral Brown, whose name has become famous in these countries. A series of combats on land and sea continued for a year and a half; and amongst the victories more celebrated than others, were those gained by the land forces over the Brazilians at Juncal and Ituzaingo. In 1828, the belligerents, somewhat exhausted, accepted the mediation of Great Britain; and by the treaty of peace that ensued, the Oriental province of Uruguay was declared a state, sovereign and independent. The Constituent Assembly, by which the Republic was formally constituted, met at Montevideo on the 18th of July, 1830.

It was at this period that a man rose into note in the Argentine Confederation, who was destined to exercise an overshadowing and pernicious influence on both sides of the River Plate. In 1829 Don Juan Manuel Rosas became governor of Buenos Aires. Possessed of great capacity, he maintained tranquillity in his native province, and extended his sway over the neighbouring states of the Confederation; but his system of government was despotic; and his rule was for some years one of terror. His reputed ambition to force the State of Paraguay into the Argentine Confederation involved him in a war with Brazil. His intervention in the intestine quarrels of the Republic of Uruguay, and his attempt to close the River Paraná to foreign vessels, led him into hostilities with England and France; whose joint naval squadrons protected Montevideo from his attacks by sea, whilst his troops and their Oriental allies under General Oribe besieged the city. The siege of Montevideo by the *Blancos* or *Whites,* as the Oriental partizans of Oribe were called, continued for nine years; and for that period, from 1842 to 1851, the history of the Republic of Uruguay is the history of the defence of Montevideo; chiefly supported by Italian legionaries under General Garibaldi, and French Basques under the command of native officers, together with the few troops the nominal government or inside party — the *Colorados* — or *Reds,* could muster. Oribe, during the war between the Argentines and Brazilians, was attacked by the Oriental cavalry of the Red party under General Flores, assisted by the Brazilian infantry, and surrendered in October 1851. On the 3rd of February in the following year, Rosas himself was completely overthrown at Monte Caseros, near Buenos Aires, by the combined forces of Brazil and the Argentines in revolt under the Governor of Entre-rios, General Justo José Urquiza. From that date, when the normal intercourse of Montevideo with Buenos Aires and the riverain ports of the Uruguay and Paraná, as well as with the interior of the Republic itself, and with Brazil, was resumed, the Banda Oriental may be said to have recommenced its national existence. Whilst her material progress has continued with little intermission, her political history during the last twenty or thirty years has been again chequered by many internal troubles, and domestic events, as yet too recent or too insignificant to be included in the present historical sketch. The old parties, the *Blancos* and *Colorados* have long since disappeared; and if, as occurs in all countries, other rivalries and other political parties have taken their place, the same bitter, and even savage animosities of an older period no longer exist; the constant communication with Europe, and the general influence of a newer education and of different ideas, is permeating all classes in the capital, and gradually extending to the rural districts, where foreigners are introducing the habits and industrial methods of European countries.

[1] See also 'Population Statistics,'.
[2] The aborigines were a yellow-skinned Indian tribe, a branch of the Pampa race of Indians, and called Charrúas.
[3] Report of the *Cabildo,* or Municipality of Montevideo, to the Viceroy, 1787. The authors of the 'Album de la Republica Oriental del Uruguay' (1882), who print the report verbatim, are of opinion that it has been published for the first time in that work. The account given therein of the productions of the country in the time of the early Spanish settlers differs essentially from the less favourable facts and opinions recorded in encyclopaedias and other English works in which the history of Uruguay is treated.

The Capital

Montevideo, the seat of government and capital of the Republic of Uruguay, was originally built on the seaward and narrower end of a small cape, or as it is sometimes called, a peninsula, at the. mouth of the River Plate; an estuary where, at this point, the water is salt, as it is for many miles further up, in the direction of Buenos Aires,

About half way towards the inland extremity of the cape, where it begins to widen, there existed till quite recently the remains of the citadel of the first Spanish colonists, and of the gateway and walls of the old city.

The principal public buildings, and the more important and business portions of Montevideo, are still within the boundaries of the old walls, but of late years the city has gradually extended over the wider part of the cape, and on to the main land. According to the plans formally laid out by the municipal authorities, in parallel lines of streets, arranged at right angles to one another, and enclosing blocks or squares of regular dimensions, Montevideo will in course of a few years spread over a very large area; and from its picturesque and healthy situation, open on two sides to the sea, and in other directions bounded by hill and stream and grassy plains, it should have scarcely a rival in South America as a place of residence.

As a question of latitude, Montevideo lies a few miles to the south of the city of Buenos Aires, the capital of the Argentine Republic, on the opposite side of the estuary. The distance east and west between the two ports is about 120 miles. The width of the river from Montevideo to Point Las Piedras, on the Argentine coast, is 53 miles. At the mouth, from "cape to cape," that is, from Cape St. Mary on the sea-coast of the Banda Oriental, to Cape St. Anthony, on the coast of the province of Buenos Aires, the River Plate is 150 miles wide.

The population of the city of Montevideo in 1879 was 91,167. The environs contained 19,000 inhabitants; giving a total population of 110,167. The population may be just double what it was twenty years ago; but owing to the late commercial crisis, which has not been confined to these countries, but has been universal, it was rather less in 1879 than some five or six years before that period.

On entering the bay, or harbour, of Montevideo, the most prominent object is the *Cerro,* or "Mount," from which the city takes its name. The bay is supposed to have once formed the crater of a volcano, and is shaped like a horse-shoe. To the left, the Cerro, surmounted by an old fort and a lighthouse, rises 505 feet, and faces the white turrets and domes of the city to the right, clustering round the cathedral placed on a slight elevation.

From the Cerro towards the land, the outline of the shore rapidly falls, but again rises gently at the *Cerrito,* or "Little Mount," a slight eminence some distance from the beach, and five or six miles from the city. It is celebrated as the head-quarters of General Oribe, the commander of the forces besieging Montevideo for nine years — from 1842 to 1851.

In the hollow of the bay the land is low, but well wooded by orchards, and studded with the *quintas,* or suburban residencies, of the citizens of Montevideo.

Part of the shore of the bay has been enclosed by a sea-wall or embankment, which forms one of the many new and delightful promenades in the environs of the capital.

Towards the Cerro, docks have been recently erected, capable of receiving sea-going vessels of heavy tonnage. There are other docks nearer to the city.

The warehouses, the wharves, the shipping of the port, and the lofty custom-house buildings, produce a favourable impression on landing. In its general characteristics, Montevideo is perhaps more European than any city in South America. Viewed at a distance, it rather resembles Cadiz in respect to its position, and the flat roofs of the houses with their turrets, or *miradores,* as they are called by the inhabitants. On nearer inspection, its symmetrical blocks of one or two-storeyed buildings, are not quite so imposing. The streets, well paved — but to Regent-street notions roughly paved — run at right angles to one another. The private houses, mostly of one storey, [1] with one wide entrance, and the windows protected by iron bars, or *rejas,* sometimes gilded and ornamented, but generally plainly painted, have a somewhat monotonous aspect. To a visitor from Northern Europe, the ground plans of the houses have, nevertheless, a novel as well as an archaeological interest. Within a very little, the several parts of a Montevidean dwelling of the better class, answer to the *vestibulum, ostium* and *atrium,* of an ancient Roman villa. In the middle of the courtyard or patio is a cistern or *aljibe.* The *patio* is often filled with flowering plants and shaded by vines, and during the summer days by an awning, and is adorned by fountains and statuary. The favourite flower, which grows to great perfection, is the Cape Jessamine; but the rose, the camellia, the magnolia, violets and carnations, and other familiar flowers of the temperate zone, as well as those of the regions bordering on the tropics, flourish in abundance; some of them flowering nearly all the year round in the suburbs of the city.

The Exchange, or *Bolsa,* in Montevideo, as well as the *Solis,* theatre or Opera House, the London and River Plate Bank, and some other of the foreign banks, are fine edifices — such as might be met with in any of the great cities of Europe; but the newly-arrived Englishman in his first loiter in Montevideo will perhaps feel that he is abroad. During the heat of the day he will not find in the streets of the city the bustle and activity of London or Liverpool. Still, when the sun is setting behind the Cerro, when the towers of the city, and the shipping in the harbour, and the bay itself, are enlivened by the evening glow and tints of the climate, a certain stir commences quite in keeping with metropolitan gaiety and pretensions.

It is then that the river steamers take their departure for Buenos Aires or the ports of the Paraná and Uruguay. The citizens, released from business, begin to wend their way on foot, or by tram or rail, to the *Paso Molino,* the *Union,* or some other resort in the suburbs; or they flock to the mole to see the passengers embark; or to the *Plaza,* or central square, where stands the cathedral, or *Matriz* as it is called. The plaza is unpretending, but prettily planted; and if not so fashionable a promenade as in other days when there were fewer attractions in the suburbs, the regimental bands play there at stated hours on Sundays and holidays, to a bright-looking and well-dressed throng of listeners. A more questionable holiday attraction — the bull-ring — is at a little distance outside the city, and approached by the *Paseo* 18 *de Julio,* once familiarly known as the *Calle Ancha* — broad street — leading to the lanes that still exist bordered by those emblems of the country, the cactus and the tall aloe. Here and there in former days there might be seen in the lanes a cross, or a little sanctuary with its light burning, in memory of some victim to accidents, recalling lawless times now fast falling out of the recollection of the present generation.

At night, the leading streets of the city are brilliantly lit, and crowded with the ladies of Montevideo, who "shop" in the evenings, and are deservedly famed for their good looks and perfect toilettes.

A lounge at one of the clubs — English, French, or native; an evening call at a friend's house according to the custom of the country; a visit to the theatre or the opera; a ball — public or private, or a midnight stroll along the shore of the bay or by the waves of the Atlantic, concludes the traveller's first day at Montevideo.

Altogether, the capital of the Republic is only too attractive to the stranger who comes to better his condition by hard work; and whose true destination is, generally speaking, the open country, or "camp," as it is called locally, on the borders of the Plata.

It cannot be too often repeated that only two classes of emigrants are fitted for the New World: those who are accustomed to manual labour — either as agriculturists, household servants, farm labourers, or as mechanics — or those who have capital to invest.

Clerks and penmen should know to whom, and in what fixed capacity they are going. Nondescripts and loafers occasionally find their way to Montevideo as to other places in the New World; but their end is the same — speedy and unfortunate.

The city of Montevideo is intersected by ram ways; and is, of course, the centre of the interior network of railways in operation or in course of construction; and the local centre of telegraphic communication with most parts of the world. It is not only the chief port of the River Plate and its tributaries, but is a convenient place of call for steamships or vessels on their way to the Pacific, or to the West Coast of South America, round Cape Horn, or through the Straits of Magellan.

There is a resident English chaplain at Montevideo; and the church is spacious and handsome. The ordinary service is Anglican; but the building is open to other Protestant denominations. The chaplain generally receives pupils; and the ceremony of confirmation is performed periodically by the Bishop of the Falkland Islands. The English cemetery is prettily placed, some little distance beyond the walls of the old city. The State religion of the Republic is Roman Catholic; but tolerance on this subject is complete and universal. The city has its public libraries and museum; and the port being in daily communication with Europe, by steam or telegraph, the residents are thoroughly conversant with the politics and doings of the rest of the world. The native families of the better class are well educated and refined. The younger members of a Montevidean household generally speak English.

"The police of the capital" says Mr. Monson, the British Minister [2] at Montevideo, in a recent report, "are efficient, vigilant, and polite; and for a seaport of importance, swarming with seafaring men of every nation in the world, and well supplied with taverns in which ardent spirits are to be procured at a comparatively low cost, public order is wonderfully well preserved. Indeed, strangers on arrival almost invariably express themselves as struck with the decorum and good behaviour of the circulating population; and in this eulogy I myself, after nearly three years' residence in the town, am bound to concur. Nor can it be said that the liberty of the individual is not, in general, respected; although upon this point I shall shortly have something further to say. As for taxation, if the imposts are heavy they are so far fairly apportioned that no one apparently escapes them; and although import duties are high, and articles of foreign origin consequently dear, the absolute necessaries of life are abundant and cheap, and there is little real poverty in the country. The press is absolutely uncontrolled, and enjoys a liberty which has, I fear, in too many cases, degenerated into an abuse."

[1] Houses with two storeys are called houses with *altos.* They are, unhappily, so much looked upon as signs of progress, that in official statistics the houses are thus classified: — houses with one storey, 8238; houses with *altos,* 2133. The old Spanish style of house with open courtyard is more healthy, and in all respects more suited to the climate.
[2] The Hon. Edmund T. Monson, C.B., Minister Resident and Consul-General.

The Rural Districts

The most northerly point of the Republic is physical nine degrees from the tropics. The extent of the country in a northerly direction varies from under two to a little under five degrees. There is not, therefore, any striking variety of climate; and with the exception that the northern provinces, or departments, are more mountainous, and that in the neighbourhood of the river Uruguay and its affluents the country is more thickly wooded, there is not much alteration to be noticed in its general character of an undulating and grassy plain, with here and there *monte,* or low woods and brushwood, and always an abundance of water.

The hilly districts in the north and east contain minerals of many kinds, including gold, lead, copper, agate, amethysts, and marble. But so far, the attempts that have been made to utilise the mineral wealth of the country have yielded poor results. Within the last two or three years, however, new companies have been formed in Europe, to work the gold-mines of Cuñapirú in Tacuarembó. On this subject the report of the British Minister already alluded to contains the following remarks: —

"I have made a casual allusion to the goldmines at Cuñapirú in another report, and before quoting, as I propose to do, the little that Dr. de Pena says upon this subject, I may as well state that the belief in their eventual success is not general in Montevideo.

"Mr. Lettsom, formerly Her Majesty's Chargé-d'affaires in this country, and himself a very accomplished geologist, took a great deal of pains years ago to investigate the auriferous capacity of the region in question, with the result, I believe, of convincing himself, and some eminent English mining engineers who were interested in the matter, that the mines could not be worked at a profit.

"Dr. de Pena writes as follows:—

"'A French company and others formed in the country have undertaken the exploration and working of the gold-mines of Cuñapirú, in the department of Tacuarembó. The French company, after various studies and assays, is making preparations to organise thoroughly this year all its machinery and laboratories. It is calculated that a capital of more than 3,000,000 dollars has already been sunk by this company; and it will require 1,500,000 dollars more to complete the preparatory works for the undertaking, which now offers employment to 1000 workmen, having contributed to form a population of 3000 inhabitants in the gold region.'

"In the report addressed to the Minister of Finance on the 27th October, 1881, by the superintendent of mines, the engineer Don Florencio Michaelson says: —

"'Two companies are working in the districts of Cuñapirú and Corrales — the "Company of the Gold-mines of Uruguay" and that of the "Gold-mines of Corrales." The first is the most important. It possesses concessions extending over more than 3600 superficial hectares, and is projecting the acquisition of new mines. Various shafts have been sunk in the concession Santa Ernestina; one of them having a depth of forty-four metres. There is a net-work of subterranean galleries, of more than 1600 metres in length. There are also several open-air workings.

"'The quantity of auriferous quartz extracted is not considerable, as is the case in the ordinary preliminary works; 200 operatives are employed on this concession, and in the neighbourhood of the principal mine there has sprung up a village of about 400 inhabitants.

"'At a league distant from Santa Ernestina, and upon the left bank of the Cuñapirú, there has lately been erected an engine-house capable of crushing in twenty-four hours 150 tons of mineral. The machinery will be set in motion by hydraulic power. A steam-engine is being set up which, when completed, will grind 30 tons daily.

"'There are at present working in Cuñapirú 400 operatives, and the population of the place is 600.

"'The "Gold-mines Company of Corrales" has concessions of a superficial extent of 2425 hectares, and it is wonderful how much it has done in a few months with only seventy labourers. It has extracted more than

1600 tons of mineral. The machinery for the engine-house is expected shortly, the masonry work being already erected on the left bank of the Corrales.

"'For both companies the past winter has been disastrous. It has been impossible to transport even one load of machinery from Salto, and at this moment the cost of trans, port is 90 dollars per 1300 kilog.'

"The last sentence indicates the real difficulty which, as I believe, will prevent these mines from ever being worked at a profit by the existing companies. That gold is to be found in tolerable quantities at Cuñapirú is certain; but the expenses of transport and of all the preliminaries will have exhausted all the capital which the companies can raise before the mines get into fair working order, and even then the distance from the port of shipment, and the cost of land-carriage, will swallow up all the profits."

None of the *sierras,* or mountains, in the Banda Oriental exceed 2000 feet in elevation; but they loom high When seen from the plains; and their tawny-coloured sides at certain seasons contrast effectively with the bright green of the glens, and the purple of the thistle flower. They are ramifications of a range of hills which, parting from the Andes in about latitude 20°, reaches the frontier of Uruguay at 32° of latitude and 56° of longitude. Here the chain divides; forming what is known as the Cuchilla de Haedo, on the north and west of the Banda Oriental, and the Cuchilla Grande to the south and east. In the provinces of Minas and Maldonado, the second range takes the name of the "Ghost Mountains." Their geological formation varies, but in the north it is chiefly gneiss and granite; and in other parts, porphyry and sandstone. The myrtle, rosemary, acacia, mimosa, and *ceibo,* with its attractive scarlet flower, exist in the sheltered clefts of the steep and stony hill sides: and a large kind of twisted thorn is so abundant, that the mountain paths are sometimes impassable. The valleys intersected by streams are fragrant with aromatic plants — myrtles and laurels of different species; and as in the plains below, the swards are often gay with the scarlet and white verbena and other wild flowers of brilliant hues. But the hills, like most other parts of the land, are devoid of luxuriant vegetation in the shape of timber and native forest. The absence of trees in that sense in the Banda Oriental is a phenomenon which even Darwin failed to account for. The same defect in the pampas on the opposite coast, is perhaps less curious. The geological formation is on that side distinct in many respects; although the pastoral wealth of both countries is due to the fertilising constituents of the *légamo pampero,* or "pampa mud," which appears historically or geologically connected with the *megatherium, mastodon, mylodon, glyptodon* and other animals, whose fossil skeletons have been found abundantly in these regions. The Jiving representative of some of these antediluvian giants is a small creature, a species of armadillo, called the *mulita,* which is found in the plains of Uruguay.

The grass is less nutritious in those departments of the Banda Oriental where the pampa mud or clay is found in its original purity. The best lands are where it exists modified by greater proportions of calcareous and siliceous material; or with less of its characteristic base, aluminum, that endows it with cold and humid qualities. Where it prevails under the best conditions, is in the departments of Soriano, in portions of Paysandú, in Durazno and in parts of Tacuarembó. Then follow Salto, other parts of Paysandú, Cerro-largo, and parts of Maldonado. It exists in equally favourable conditions in certain valleys and localities in the other departments.

The climate and soil of the Republic are capable of producing nearly every description of semi-tropical and European productions; but it may be said frankly, that the State of Uruguay is not yet peopled. One-fourth of the soil is still even without ownership. It belongs nominally to the Government, but is not yet surveyed.

Under these circumstances, and considering the general characteristics of the country — consisting of streams with thinly wooded banks, and of vast tracts of undulating pasture land, with here and there a white estancia house, surrounded by a patch of newly planted trees, it can be anticipated that the riches of the country consist mainly of flocks and herds. The principal exports are hides, horns, tallow, and wool. Cattle-rearing is the chief industry, and more than any other in the hands of the natives. It requires more land but less labour than agriculture; and will prosper on coarser land, but requires perhaps more local and special knowledge than sheep-feeding.

It cannot be said that the natives succeed better than Englishmen or other foreigners in the management of a cattle estancia; but the *peones* or native labourers are from their infancy trained to the use of the *lasso* and to the handling of horses and cattle that a few years ago were in many parts allowed to roam wild about the vast tracts of land which some of the larger estancias will often cover.

At the present day, the cattle industry, like everything else in the interior of the Republic, is influenced by the existing state of transition from the semi-barbarous freedom or lawlessness of a thinly peopled and pastoral country to a condition similar to that of an English colony, where the competition of skilled European labour, and the introduction of capital, have effected a revolution in the ruder means formerly employed in the rearing either of sheep or cattle in young countries.

That the cattle industry has always been considered the chief industry in the Banda Oriental is easily accounted for; since, if on an estancia we take the usual proportion of sheep to cattle as 5 to 1, the relative value of the cattle one with another as compared to that of the sheep is as 6 to 1. There is probably no country in the world, not even the neighbouring Argentine Republic, so rich in herds of cattle as the Republic of Uruguay, whether we estimate the number in proportion to population or to extent of territory. In 1878 the proportion was calculated at 32.60 head of cattle per square kilometre and 1385 per cent, of the population. The sheep were calculated at 65.2 per kilometre and 2770 per cent, of the population. In the wealthy province of Buenos Aires, in the neighbouring Republic, the calculations were, in regard to sheep, 215.3 per kilometre, and 8275 per cent, of the population, but the cattle were only in the proportion of 930 head per cent. of the population, and 24.2 per square kilometre.

The rearing of cattle is undoubtedly attended with great risks, owing to its dependence on good seasons. Disease and droughts will lower the condition and selling value of the animals, even if they do not destroy them by hundreds. The droughts are more fatal to cattle than to sheep.

The old difficulties in the rearing of cattle in South American countries, when the animals were running nearly wild, were the catching, branding, and counting. For some of these purposes the herds were driven to what is called a *rodeo,* some convenient and well-worn spot on an estate, where they were surrounded by *peones,* or *gauchos* as the native peasantry or herdsmen are called, who, well mounted on the small but active horses of the country, and armed with the *lasso* and *bolas,* would ride round the herd, and keep the refractory from straying whilst the animals were counted or branded, or points of the better-conditioned were selected and parted for sale.

The calves were branded as soon as possible, to prevent them from wandering into the herds on other estates where they were liable to be claimed by the neighbours. The usual time for marking cattle is in the autumn, when the season is temperate and suited to the more rapid healing of the wounds inflicted by the hot irons.

In the northern provinces, and in other parts of the country, the cattle are still wild, and the rough-and-ready native methods of treating them are yet adhered to; but the gradual introduction of a newer system of adopting wire fencing and of erecting sheds, cattle "races," and various inclosures, is effecting a complete revolution in the cattle industry itself, as well as in the appearance and moral characteristics of some of the rural departments. It is not yet safe to expend capital in too many modem improvements until the consumption of the country and other markets more clearly determine what is required in the way of the breed and condition of the animals. At the present time it may be calculated that over a million and a half of cattle are consumed annually. Of these more than half a million are killed simply for the tallow and hides they produce for export4 The beef of the country, as it is cooked in a primitive manner in the rural districts, on an *azada* or large iron spit, is wholesome and excellent, but tough because eaten in general freshly killed. There is as yet no attempt made on any extended scale at rearing animals for the butcher or for the dairy, as in countries where agriculture, pursued as a science, exists side by side with pastoral pursuits, and where populous towns and easy means of communication supply ready markets. What is done to a large extent is to winter — *invernar* — cattle; that is, when the summer, the killing season at the *saladeros,* is over, lean oxen are purchased at low prices, 8 to 10 dollars each, and allowed to fatten on good lands during the winter, and are sold in the spring in Montevideo, or to the extract of meat factories at 15 or 17 dollars each, and even at higher prices. The different inventions for facilitating the export of meat, either in hermetically sealed tins, or chemically prepared, or in refrigerated chambers, are certainly destined before long to enormously increase and improve the cattle industry in Uruguay. At present the refrigerating process, which a newly-formed English company is now establishing at Colonia to work the Haslam patent, is confined to the freezing of mutton.

Closely connected with the rearing of cattle are the great establishments called *saladeros,* or killing grounds, at the different ports, where the hides and tallow are prepared for shipment to Europe. In the neighbourhood of Montevideo there are nine *saladeros;* and on the River Uruguay ten — including the large establishment belonging to the "Liebig Extract of Meat Company," at Fray Bentos. This employs 400 or 500 men, and loads at its own wharves upwards of eighty vessels during the year for the export of the produce to Europe.

In the Department of Cerro Largo there are three *saladeros,* and in the Department of San José is the meat-preserving establishment of Messrs. Herrera and Co.; and at Paysandu Messrs. J. McCall and Co.'s establishment.

The number of cattle killed at the *saladeros* each year — or in each *faena,* as the killing season is called — often exceeds 600,000, of which number nearly 150,000 are used for the Liebig extract.

Besides a vast number of sheep, 60,000 to 80,000 mares are killed annually at the *saladeros.* The hides, tallow, grease, and other products of these establishments involve the turning over annually of 2½ to 3 millions sterling.

The commercial value of an ox, young and in good condition, can be gathered from the following figures: —

Hide, 68 lbs., at 71 rials p. 75 lbs. ..	$6·43
Tallow, 40 lbs., at 13 rials p. 25 lbs. ..	2·04
Meat, 150 lbs., at 55 rials *fuertes* per quintal of 100 lbs.	9·90
Remnants	50
	$18·87 = 4*l.* sterling.

The saladero expenses for each animal are about $3.60. [1]

The mode of killing cattle and the general process of work in a *saladero* has often been described, but one of the latest accounts is in Mr. Ph. H. Rathbone's report to the *Prange Estancia Company,* Liverpool, whose property, *Nueva Alemania,* is beautifully situated on the banks of the river Uruguay, a little south of the town of Soriano, in the department of that name.

North of Soriano, on the coast, and formerly in the department of Paysandu, but now in the new department of Rio Negro, is Fray Bentos, where the Liebig Extract is made, and the methods and nature of the work at the saladeros and manufactories of that establishment are thus described by Mr. Rathbone. He says: — "Next morning, about six o'clock, I went down to the *galpon,* or shed, and found them just beginning to kill. The cattle are, on arrival, driven into large *corrales,* or paddocks, arranged so as to supply them with water, but no food is given to them. A long, narrow passage, about six or seven feet wide, and skirted by a long, narrow platform pathway about the height of the animals' horns, leads down to a small oval paddock, with a similar pathway around and a bridge over the opening into the *galpon,* which is further closed by a movable beam. Below the bridge is a large, low, square iron truck on a tramway, which runs into the *galpon,* and branches described into two parallel lines, so that two trucks may pass each other. Along the left side of the shed are long ranges of rails for hanging meat; and along the right hand, a flat, slightly shelving, flagged space, for laying the oxen upon. At the end of the shed is a large brine bath for soaking the skins, and beyond this there are further sheds where the skins are piled up with salt previous to being shipped. In *saladeros* the skins are generally salted, but on *estamias* the hides are usually dried. As I arrived, about fifty oxen were being hunted down the "race" or passage into the fatal paddock. They seemed to have an instinct of what was to follow, for there was a peculiar scared look about many of them. I have been told that when on an *estancia* any animal is killed for consumption, the herd gather around the body and moan. When the paddock was full and the gate shut, a man with a *lasso,* of which one end was attached to a steam winch outside (natives call it the "English horse"), went round the pathway and threw the noose over the most prominent horns he could see, which were by no means ordinarily the nearest to the bridge. The winch being set going, the beast was hauled, stumbling and slipping and pushing aside all animals in its way, till its head was chocked up against the upper beam leading into the *galpon,* upon which stood the killer, who with a stab close behind the head with a large dagger-bladed knife cut the spinal cord, and the animal at once dropped with a heavy thud, but without a struggle, on to the iron truck. The lower beam was then rapidly withdrawn, the *lasso* disengaged, and the truck run into the *galpon* by two men. Here, by means of a *lasso* attached to a horse, the animal was hitched into its place at the side of the shed, where a skinner was waiting for it, who immediately cut its throat and began to skin it. The blood was caught in large scoops and ladled into casks placed for the purpose. Meanwhile the skinner rapidly took the skin off, and though sensation was probably entirely destroyed by severance of the spinal cord, yet muscular action was not, and it was rather ghastly to see the struggles of an animal with half its skin off, and even detect a sound painfully like a bellow. These movements seemed to take place when certain nerves were touched about the neck, and thus set in action. The skin off, it was taken to the brine bath spoken of. The entrails were taken out and carried away, the ribs cleared of flesh, and the limbs cut off and taken to the opposite side of the *galpon,* and there all the meat was cut from the bones, and hung up on the rails provided for that purpose, together with that cut off the ribs, &c., still warm and quivering with life. The skull and horns were taken in a different direction. This operation takes from eight to nine minutes on an average, but on occasions has been done in five, and the skinner waits his next turn, which comes every fifteen minutes. As the truck is run out, the alternative truck is run into the paddock, and the beam shot back for another victim.

"The shed contains about twenty-five oxen at a time, so that about a hundred are killed, skinned, and cut up in an hour, and in the height of the killing season as many as twelve hundred are thus disposed of per diem, or from 100,000 to 150,000 a season. Each skinner gets sixpence per head, but if, in skinning, he makes a hole in the skin, he loses his payment for that animal. In the height of the season he disposes of about 33 in a day. Not unfrequently the horns of the one lassoed become entangled with the horns of another, and they are brought up to the beam and despatched together; and though I did not see it, I heard that even three are sometimes thus brought up. During the time the beam is drawn back a frightened beast often makes a dart for it, and sometimes gets through into the *galpon,* and goes plunging along it, clearing the place of every one in it, and at times ends by going headlong into the brine skin bath, from which it has to be fished out with *lassoes* as best may be. There are two men always ready with *lassoes* to intercept it if possible before this happens. The morning I was there no animal got more than its head and shoulders through, but even when this happened all got ready for a prompt disappearance out of the place. After a hundred and fifty were disposed of in an hour and a half, the remainder were left till after breakfast, and the place was cleaned up in a marvellously short time, making it difficult to believe that such a scene of blood bad been taking place so recently. This is explained by every skinner being responsible for cleaning up the square he occupies. A similar number were killed in the same way and time after breakfast.

"When it has cooled, the meat is cleared of fat, and is stewed in large oblong caldrons, in which the water is kept somewhat below boiling-point, as it is a peculiarity of the Extract that it contains no matter which is not soluble in cold as distinguished from boiling water. The thin soup so obtained is then strained off, and carefully skimmed, which removes any trace of grease that may have remained in the meat. It is then passed through a series of elaborate evaporators, out of each of which it comes thicker until it reaches a consistency rather more solid than treacle. As much as 90,000 gallons of water a day is sometimes thus evaporated. It is now ready for use, and is packed in large cube tins holding about 110 lbs. of the Extract. Each of these tins contains, on an average, the substance of fifteen animals, and is worth about 50*l*. The tins are exported in that form to Europe, where the contents are subdivided to suit consumers...

"There is a large tin-shop where the various tins are made, with very effective machinery for cutting, stamping, or bending the metal as required. There is also a carpenter's and engineer's shop— each on a very complete scale; also a day-school for the children of the workmen. The establishment is therefore very complete within itself; and not the least interesting is the laboratory, where experiments are made and processes tested under the care of trained scientific men, so as to secure the best and most uniform results. The refuse, blood, &c. — when there is killing — escapes into the river Uruguay, and attracts innumerable swarms of fish, some being of most singular species, and there is plenty of fishing off the quay. I am told that in the height of the season the water is perfectly alive with the masses of fishes' heads visible above the surface, and that it is a wonderful sight. It is, however, not so much so as formerly, because more of the refuse is now saved and made use of.

"In fact, the utmost seems to be made of everything, and a careful finish, completeness, and cleanliness characterises every operation. This could only have been attained by a constant watchfulness over every detail, and a succession of small improvements and economies."

More than a hundred years ago, in 1778, it was stated, in official documents still extant, that there existed in the Banda Oriental "numerous herds of wild cattle." A carcass, according to Azara, was then worth sixpence, and a young ox half-a-crown. About the years 1792 to 1796 the annual export of dry hides was 758,117. In the years 1841 and 1842 the exports of dry and salted hides were about 1,244,301. In 1860 there were 5,218,700 head of cattle in the country, which had been nearly swept clean of livestock in the great war 1842-51. The extraordinary increase was due to the impetus given by the sale for export owing to the gradual establishment of the *saludero* industry and the introduction of the process of salting hides on a larger scale, which raised the price of cattle.

The increase in late years has not continued in the same ratio, and the annual slaughter at the *saladeros* varies from one year to another.

In the year 1881 the *faena* of the *saladeros* was deficient on account of the dry season, but even in spite of the want of rain and the consequent poor condition of the pasture, there were slaughtered 576,170 head of cattle; whilst in the neighbouring Argentine Republic they killed only 399,000 head; showing a difference of 44 per cent, in favour of Uruguay.

The agriculture of the country is still in its infancy, but makes rapid progress. [2] About 600,000/fanegas [3] of wheat, and 266,000 fanegas of Indian corn were produced annually from 1870 to 1878; which is just triple the quantity produced in the years 1855 to 1860, and could be increased to any extent, but at present, pasturage is more remunerative. In the Report of the Ministry of Finance published in 1882, the annual produce of agriculture in the Republic is valued at six millions of dollars; or about 1,270,000*l*.

In certain districts, and in a few large rural departments where agriculture is attended to, machinery of all kinds is gradually being adopted; and around the *estancia* houses, the eucalyptus, the mulberry, the olive and vine, are carefully cultivated.

An interesting feature in the agriculture of these countries are the so-called *Colonies* —meaning agricultural settlements or communities, composed of the poorer class of European immigrants, principally Swiss, Waldenses, and Spaniards, the latter from the Canary Islands.

The Swiss settlement was founded in 1862, It has an area of 4 square leagues, divided into *chacras,* or farms of 20 *cuadras,* or squares, each. [4] The farms border on the public roads of the community. Each proprietor has to cede 6 yards of land for the construction of the roads, 12 yards wide. The Piedmontese settlement was founded in 1858, and is the most populous and productive.

The original prices of the farms, or *chacras,* were 40*l*. each, or about 21*s*. 10*d*. the acre.

The population of the Colony — which eighteen years ago commenced with a handful of half-disconsolate and disappointed but sturdy immigrants — had risen in 1878 to 5130. The Swiss number 1700. The Piedmontese, 1870; and the Canary Islanders, 1200. A few English, Germans, and immigrants from other countries, form the remainder.

The community is in all respects complete, having its proper complement of artisans, mechanics, and commercial agents. Each religious denomination has its own chaplain; and as far as purely local questions are concerned, the community governs itself. It possesses reading-rooms, clubs, musical societies, and a Swiss rifle association; and seems, in good harmony, to prosper by hard work and the sale of its wheat and Indian corn, eggs, poultry, butter, potatoes, beans, and most descriptions of vegetables.

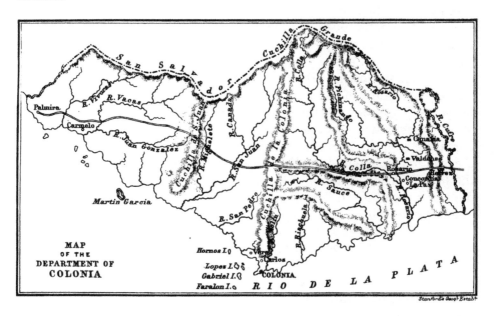

It has lately produced large quantities of cheese — promising to be an important article of export; and is rich in fruits of all kinds.

including pears, that in the Banda Oriental, and particularly in the neighbourhood of Montevideo, are noted for their excellence, and are considered nearly equal to the pears of France or Jersey, The Colony produces, also, apples, cherries, plums, apricots, peaches, nuts, oranges, lemons, figs, currants, filberts, grapes, and chestnuts. [5]

In an agricultural establishment of the kind, where men are not isolated, and where, working as proprietors on their own behalf, they have the use of mechanical appliances, and enjoy the moral and, if needs be, the physical aid and all the social advantages of the general community around them — they and their families can be happy, and relatively wealthy, when cultivating comparatively a few acres; whereas, if engaged in the rearing of. cattle, they would require thirty or forty times more land — one square league at least — and even if prosperous, would probably lead a somewhat barbarous existence.

The three colonies, Swiss, Piedmontese, and Spanish are situated in the *Rincon del Rey,* in the department of Colonia, not far from the shore of the River Plate, and cover an area of about 14 leagues, near the inland port of Rosario, on a navigable river of the same name. These agricultural communities are not much to the taste of an average Englishman; and clash, or appear to clash, with superstitions he has imbibed in his own country, when living under an agricultural system essentially distinct. Still, English settlements abroad have lately been projected— in some respects resembling the agricultural "colonies" of the Plate. And of all systems of emigration on a large scale, it seems as if the method of colonising by settlements or communities, will eventually prove the most efficient. The fact is, the clever and the robust may get on without mutual assistance anywhere, and under most ordinary circumstances; but the good conferred by a few clever persons on the countries of their adoption is partial or sporadic, whilst the men themselves are a serious loss to the old countries they abandon. What is wanted in new countries are *numbers;* and men and women with ordinary capacities willingness to work steadily,' and a tendency to remain permanently.

The question of agricultural colonies is always under the notice of the larger landed proprietors, who have made plans for the subdivision of their estates; and in 1880 the subject was taken up by the legislature, and a new "Colonial Law" was passed in June 1881. The word "Colony" or "Colonial," in the sense here used, is of course misapplied, and has its origin in the history of the country; when under the dominion of the Spaniards, the waste lands and frontiers were partially colonised as a military protection against the Indians. In the sense of "settlements" there are other colonies existing in different parts of the Republic; amongst the rest, that of "New Berlin," a German settlement or establishment created by Messrs. Wendelstadt and Co., on the banks of the Uruguay, about ten leagues from Fray Bentos.

In some of the northern departments of the Republic, government land can be purchased at 2*s.* an acre. In *Cerro Largo,* bordering on Brazil, farms or plots of land of 20 *cuadras* each can be had for 6*l.* or 7*l.*, and the proprietors of the land will give to settlers, house, food, seeds, cattle, &c,, for the first year to work the ground "on halves." The 'Hand-book of the River Plate Republics' (from which this information is taken) says, in describing the department of *Cerro Largo*: —

"It is a fine working country, well wooded and watered, but almost in the same primeval state as when the Minuans hunted over it before the Spanish conquest. The mountain ranges are bold and picturesque; the rivers Olimar, Cebollaty, and Tacuari, could easily be made navigable from Lake Mini; the lands are of extraordinary fertility; nothing is wanted but population to turn to advantage such a splendid territory. Wherever agriculture has been tried, the results are almost fabulous, and all the products of the tropics may be raised in the open air. The woods abound in valuable timber of various kinds, and the palm-tree gracefully towers above all."

This tempting description will apply, more or less, to other districts, in the distant and almost semitropical departments of the Republic of Uruguay, as well as of its neighbour, the Argentine Republic; but in their present condition, and from the nature of their productions, they are not the districts which the individual English emigrant would choose; although they might serve for settlements.

Nearer to the River Plate, the physical characteristics of Uruguay are very similar to parts of Great Britain and Ireland; excepting that the climate has all the beauty of that of Italy or the South of France.

The settler in the southern districts is troubled neither with venomous reptiles nor dangerous beasts of prey. Such things exist; and on the borders of Brazil, and in other places, there is the tiger or ounce, as well as the puma, the lion of the country, but unless a man beats about the wooded islets or the swampy banks of the large rivers, he may pass a lifetime in most parts of Uruguay without meeting anything more formidable than a small viper [6] — such as he would see in an English hedge-row, or the harmless *carpincho,* a species of amphibious pig. On the other hand, deer, ostriches, partridges of the size of grouse — with very much of their manner on the wing — innumerable small partridges, ducks, and waterfowl of all descriptions, will afford him excellent sport.

Of the Ostriches (*Rhea Americana*), Mr. Rathbone says: "These birds are numerous, but some years ago the Government, fearing their extinction, forbade their being killed. They are of a different kind to the African ostrich; the ' Rhea is their real name. They have brown and white feathers. Each male has a number of females, who lay in the same nest, in one of which I have seen as many as fifty eggs. The male sits and hatches, leaving one or two eggs outside of the nest in the sun to addle, which when the brood is hatched are broken, and the contents attract flies, which form one of the principal sources of nourishment of the young ostriches. I was told that a contractor in Montevideo was willing to pay five reals, about 2*s.* 1*d.* per ostrich, for the privilege of plucking, which is done by cutting the feathers off close to the skin, when fresh feathers are said to grow with increased luxuriance, This contractor sends his own men, takes all management of the plucking, and pays the expenses incurred, but I am not sure whether or not he expects his men to be fed while employed. It is said that when the birds have once been plucked it is very difficult to get near them the next year, and if the camp is not well fenced they are apt to leave; also that many inconveniences arise through disturbance of flocks, &c., in hunting down the birds. The value of the feathers is about 17s. 6d. per lb. African ostrich farming is being tried in the Argentine provinces in at least one case, but the cost of the birds is a serious item, as a pair of breeding ostriches in South Africa costs about 150*l*., and though the value of their feathers is enormous, and the demand very large, yet from the nature of their use as mere ornaments, the continuance of the demand must be very precarious. The climate appears to be very favourable to this industry."

In many respects, the Banda Oriental compares favourably with the flourishing Buenos province of Buenos Aires, on the opposite side of the River Plate. The cattle in Uruguay are larger, and produce a finer flavoured beef than in Buenos Aires. In proportion to the population, both cattle and sheep are more numerous; but the grass of Buenos Aires is of a much better quality, and, acre for acre, will feed many more sheep. Uruguay, however, possesses the paramount advantage of the port of Montevideo — the only really good harbour for shipping, not only in the Plate but on the whole seaboard for hundreds of miles.

Owing to the abundance of water in the interior, Uruguay suffers less than its neighbour from droughts. The country is not subject to violent storms of wind and dust; and snow-storms are unknown. Plagues of locusts, which in Buenos Aires are of frequent occurrence, have until lately happened only at long intervals in Uruguay. Until the last two or three years, for a period of twenty-five years there had been only three such visitations.

The English who possess *estancias,* or estates, in the Banda Oriental, rear large quantities of cattle for the *saladeros;* but if we take the rural departments of the Republic in the order in which they produce the greater number of sheep, it will afford to the English reader or immigrant a sufficient topographical and geographical guide, if his purpose be to ascertain the haunts of his fellow-countrymen in Uruguay; many of whom, both there and in Buenos Aires, have acquired fame for the breeds of sheep they have introduced.

On leaving the city of Montevideo, we can pass over the metropolitan department of the same name; and also the adjoining department of *Canelones,* which is, relatively speaking, an agricultural district much in the hands of foreigners — chiefly immigrants from the Canary Islands, who raise wheat and grow vegetables for the consumption of the capital. Following the map, and keeping towards the coast of the River Plate and Uruguay, we come to the department of *Colonia,* with 1,922,149 sheep; *Soriano,* with 2,033,666 sheep; *San José,* with 2,264,920; *La Florida,* with 1,546,700; and *Paysandu,* with 1,001,196. We are now far up the Uruguay towards the north-west, with only the department of *Salto* between the

Republic and Brazil. Salto, and the remaining departments to the north and east contain 300,000 to 500,000 sheep each. There is one more central province, *Durazno,* to the north of Colonia, which contains 967,000 sheep. [7]

Naturally, the immigration and population in general have spread from the metropolitan department of Montevideo — possessing nearly one-fourth of the inhabitants of the whole Republic — along the coasts of the great rivers; where the land is also better adapted to pastoral pursuits, and to sheep-feeding in particular. The department of *Tacuarembó* in the extreme north, and which is wild and mountainous, and also the largest of all the departments, contains 1,212,953 head of cattle; mostly the property of Brazilian immigrants from the neighbouring province of Eio Grande. The stock of sheep in Tacuarembó is only 508,880. The same larger proportion of cattle to sheep exists in the other departments, *Cerro Largo, Minas,* and *Maldonado* to the north and east. Livestock, The number of livestock of all kinds, cattle, sheep, mares, pigs, goats, and mules is variously estimated. In 1876 it was put down at 19,191,273, from official statistics; but in the following year from other calculations it was shown that there were at least 7,000,000 of cattle alone, and 14,000,000 of sheep. The number of sheep in 1880 is officially given at 10,536,042. Making allowances for the moderate calculations of official statistics, there is no doubt that of late years the sheep have decreased in number.

The average value of the cattle per head, and one with another, is about 6 dollars (25*s.* 6*d.*); and of the sheep, 1 dollar (4*s.* 3*d.*). Working oxen and milch-cows average 25 dollars per head (5*l.* 6*s.* 3*d.*). Cattle for the *saladeros,* 12 dollars (2*l,* 11*s.*). The compiler of the official statistics (Apuntes Estadisticos) for 1878, values the cattle of all ages at an average price of 4 dollars and 70 cents (1*l.*) per head. The number of cattle of that description he estimates at 5,192,488; cattle for the *saladeros* at 800,000; and labouring oxen and milch-cows at 100,000. The total value is placed at 36,505,603 dollars (7,767,155*l.*). The mares for the *saladeros* are valued at 10*s.* 6*d.* each; mules at 38*s.* 3*d.* each; goats at 8*s.* 6*d.*; and pigs at 25*s.* 6*d.*

Riding horses are not so cheap as they were some years ago, when a fair animal, young and pretty well trained, could be purchased for three or four pounds. They are still to be had at reasonable prices compared with their cost in England.

It is not the custom in the River Plate countries to ride mares; although innovations in that respect may have lately been introduced by foreigners, particularly Englishmen; who for many years past have introduced blood stallions, and affect horse-racing in true Newmarket fashion.

The native breed of horses was introduced by the Spaniards, and still preserves vestiges of Arab blood. Some of the animals have a pretty head and shoulders, but fall off in beauty towards the hind-quarters. Others are roman-nosed, ball-eyed, and heavy-looking; but all are hardy and active, though small, standing about fourteen hands. Ridden by natives, with native gear, and at the usual pace of the country, a gentle canter, they will travel as much as thirty leagues in a day.

The sheep industry on any large scale sheep dates only from 1855. The sheep introduced by the Spaniards in olden times in their trading ships gradually increased to flocks; but assumed a peculiar type of coarse woolled animals, still well known in the country as *criollo;* at the beginning of the century there were about two millions and a half of this class of sheep. It was not until 1832 that Señor Juanico introduced into the department of Canelones a finer Spanish breed. His example was followed in 1838, when a Frenchman imported into Colonia a flock of 300 Merinos from Naz, in France. In 1840 the famed Negretti, and in 1852 the Rambouillet rams and ewes arrived in the Republic from Europe.

From 1840 to 1842, 7,500,000 lbs. of wool were annually exported. From 1869 to 1872 the average annual export was 44,471,700 lbs. In the year 1872 itself, the exports rose to over 50,000,000 lbs.; and the phenomenon still remains unexplained that since that date the exports of wool have continued more or less stationary. Many ascribe the fact to the prevalence of bad seasons, and climatic changes which have occurred during the last ten years. Others think the secret is in the overstocking of the land in those departments of the Republic more specially devoted to sheep-feeding. The traditional methods of the country still obtain amongst the smaller sheep-farmers; and no effort is made to adopt a more scientific handling of the flocks. The avarice of the owners leads them to believe in numbers; and it is difficult to persuade them that thinning the flocks of the old ewes, and leaving only the best of the animals, will in the end, give from the reduced flock, a greater return of wool.

Now that the system of enclosing the land with fencing has become more general, and the parting of the flocks as well as the parting the cattle from the sheep, has been more attended to, a great improvement may be expected. The brilliant success of the wools of the Banda Oriental at the Wool Exhibition at the Crystal Palace in London in the summer of 1881, when they were placed side by side with the choicest specimens of wools from the British Colonies in Australasia, will no doubt give a stimulus to increased exertion; and convince the native farmers that the success of the growers in Uruguay who obtained prizes at that exhibition, was due to care and to judicious methods of crossing the breeds, so as to suit the different crosses to the special conditions of the pasture of the country and the climate.

The Exhibition of Wool and Woollen Industries at the Crystal Palace is likely to form an epoch not only in the history of sheep feeding in the Banda Oriental, but in the woollen manufacture in England itself. In his report on the exhibition to the *Asociacion Rural* of Uruguay, the Consul-General of the Republic in London pointed out, that the reason why, hitherto, so little of the wools of the River Plate countries was consumed in Great Britain, and why nearly the whole of it found its way to Havre and Antwerp, was on account of the defective machinery still obstinately employed by the manufacturers of Bradford and other seats of the British woollen manufacture.

Their machinery has been gradually adapted to work the long, clean, bright, and comparatively coarse-fibred British wools, free from the seed and vegetable matter, which from the nature of the grass in the River Plate districts. still disfigure their shorter fibred, finer, and softer Merino wools.

From the long, coarse, but lustrous Lincoln wool, the English manufacturers made a description of goods, called *lustres.* In dresses, they were bright looking, but stiff, like alpaca goods; and of late years they have gone out of fashion, and are likely to remain so, as they cannot be compared in appearance or comfort with the soft Merino goods of French and Belgian manufacture.

To work the softer but less clean Merino wools produced cheaply in the River Plate, it was necessary to invent a certain kind of carding machine. This was done in France; and the Belgians promptly adopted the invention. The astounding result in Belgium, was that whilst, from 1850 to 1855, only 11,000 bales of River Plate wool were imported, the importations increased from 1870 to 1875 to 158,000 bales; and in place of the manufacture of woollen yarn being, as in 1850, only 29,000 kilogrammes, barely sufficient for the home consumption, it so increased with the employment of the new machinery, that Belgium, in 1879, exported to England and other places, 6,588,000 kilogrammes.

Visibly, but very slowly, the subject gains the attention of the Bradford manufacturers. In the meantime, Messrs. Piatt Bros. & Co., of Oldham, Messrs. J. & W. McNaught, and Messrs. J. Petrie, of Rochdale, have invented machines which at the exhibition at the Crystal Palace could be seen combing and carding the River Plate wools into yarn, and extracting the seeds and other matter, at the rate of consumption of 1000 lbs. of wool daily.

Sooner or later the French system of carding will be general in England; and London will become a great market for River Plate wools. What arrives now, either of River Plate or Australian wool is mostly trans-shipped, and re-exported to the Continent.

The following particulars are condensed from a detailed description of the sheep, and sheep industry, in Mr. Rathbone's pamphlet.

"The sheep chiefly bred in the River Plate countries may be roughly divided into four varieties: — 1, The Native, or Criolla; 2, English; 3, Merino; and 4, Mixed, or Mestiza.

1. **Native.** These are fast disappearing. They have long straight wool, almost like hair, which is used for stuffing mattresses, cushions, &c.

2. **English.** Of these, Lincolns are the chief; but Romney Marsh and Southdown are becoming more looked after. Southdowns are better for mutton than wool, and are therefore chiefly available for the neighbourhoods of large meat markets, but might become more valuable in the event of the export of mutton; but this is not likely to take any large proportions at present. English sheep, as a rule, run larger than Merinos; their wool is not so fine, greasy, or close, and they can be shorn much quicker — though the shearers get the same sum per head as for Merinos. The wool, when washed, gives a much larger percentage of clean wool than Merinos, say English 55 to 60 per cent., and Merinos, 34 to 40 per cent. The English sheep are better nurses than the Merinos, which, when a storm comes, scamper off, leaving their lambs to take care of themselves, while an English mother will not be induced to desert her lamb. English sheep scatter in feeding, while Merino sheep feed very closely together, and it seems a question whether Merinos do not tread down the ground more than English, though the latter are supposed to eat more, being larger bodied in proportion to the weight of wool.

3. **Merino,** may be divided into Negrettis, which have been bred in Grermany from a Spanish stock, and Rambouillets, which have been bred in France. The wool is very thick, fine, and greasy in both varieties, and washes very light in comparison with English wool. The Negrettis chiefly prevail in Uruguay, and the Rambouillets are more fancied in the Argentine provinces, being for the most part of a larger body.

4. **Mestiza** are the various breeds produced by crossing the previous varieties. It is quite a question whether, by crossing, a breed of sheep may not be produced specially adapted to the climate and grass of the Plate, but the question is yet in its infancy. In Buenos Aires there are now regular ram sales, and imported English, Saxon, and Rambouillet rams are sold at high prices; besides which, in the neighbourhood of Buenos Aires, there are breeding farms, notably that of Mr. Chas, whose rams bring high prices. At a sale from his *estancia,* some months ago, fifty rams were sold for $420,600 m.c., or an average of $8412 m.c, say at $125 per £ = 67*l*. 6*s*. Some of them sold as high as 232*l*., 160*l*., 128*l*., the lowest price being 38*l*. 8*s*., but the run were 40*l*. to 80*l*.

The following extracts are quoted from 'Sheep-farming in the Banda Oriental,' a pamphlet printed some years ago for private circulation. It was written at a period immediately preceding the introduction into the Banda Oriental of railways and trams, of a more extended use of wire-fencing, and of machinery, and other European methods in pastoral as well as agricultural pursuits. But in the main, the graphic descriptions given are still applicable to estates distant from the metropolitan province; and in some parts of the country the mode of travelling described is precisely as it exists at this day. The calculations presented of the profits of an estancia might be varied in one or two items to suit the expenditure as well as the prices of produce at this time; but the facts stated are more than usually reliable. The author of the pamphlet is a large landowner in the River Plate countries, and occupies a high mercantile position in London and Buenos Aires.

The Journey

"The theatre was very well-lighted, the scenery and decorations good — all seemed at home there; and I must confess that I have seen few interiors in Europe that could rival or surpass the 'Solis' of Montevideo; and we were already half-regretting having arranged to start so quickly for the country. It was midnight when we left the theatre. We must be at the diligence office by four o'clock; so that almost before we were asleep, the black boy (to whom we had promised a dollar if he would wake us up) was pulling me, with *son las cuatro, señor.* Saddles, bridles, saddle-bags, and pouches had been sent before. We stumbled along in the dark, half-awake, to the coach-office; found we were in good time: for there stood a kind of Noah's Ark on wheels, and its accompaniment of passengers, horse-boys, and porters — something in the style of home one hundred years back.

"A cup of coffee, and in we went. Men, women, and children had their representatives. Two of the men had most formidable blunderbusses. I found afterwards they were native Estancieros — and very pleasant fellows too — who had seen sights making their arms friends in need; other two had revolvers. There was an Irishman who told me he had ten thousand sheep, and did not care a snap even for the Lord Mayor of Dublin."

The Country

"The country, after passing San José, is quite open, with an almost monotonous succession of gently-sloping hills and dales, and larger or smaller streams running at the bottom of each hollow. Where the river is large, a fringe of wood belts its course, emerging from which, yon come upon a rising hill covered to the summit with rich grass, completely clear of wood or shrub — something like the downs in the South of England, only that the pasturage is much richer, and the ground generally a black loamy soil, evidently most fertile. As we saw it then, it was most luxuriantly green — full of all colours of wild flowers: the scarlet verbena, the white campanilla, red clover, yellow and blue, indeed, all colours mingled with the green grass. Nothing could more realise the ideal of a land made for flocks and herds. The cattle grazed at will, spreading out in points over the extent of bill and dale; whilst flocks of sheep fed on the hill-sides, sprinkling the green ground with thousands of white spots. The Estancia house is always placed at the top of the most commanding hill — enabling the owner to overlook his domain, and see that his cattle are safe, and that no suspicious strollers are about." ...

The Estancia House

"I have already described the country as having a regular series of hills and dales, Whenever there was no such deep stream at the bottom of these hollows, as to altogether endanger the safety of the diligence, by passing them at full speed, the great aim of our driver seemed to be, by as rapid a descent as possible, to obtain as much impetus as would force .us half-way up to the opposite hill without any assistance from the horses. Picture to yourself, then, this heavy Noah's Ark shooting down the hillside as fast as the horses could gallop before it, our *cuarteador,* at the head of all, yelling and shouting to frighten the half-wild horses to their utmost speed; then through the hollow, when up the high ascent — where whips and oaths, and kicks on the splash-board, anything or any noise to goad the wretched team to maddened exertion — the pace gradually slackens, and the top of the hill is reached almost at a walk.

"We arrived at the end of our last stage in good time, finding horses ready, waiting to carry us on to the Estancia, which lay about fifteen miles distant from the coach road...In little more than an hour we found ourselves crossing the pass of the Perdido river, close to the Estancia house. A hospitable welcome, a well-built mansion, everything about orderly and well-arranged, and the language of home spoken on all sides, almost made us forget that we were so far away...From the *azotea* [8] of the house we had a fine view of the Estancia lands, stretching on each side for some miles. Close about the house were the farm buildings; the *galpon,* or shed, for the wool-press and shearing — in front of which are arranged the enclosures of hurdles, used for shutting-up the flocks for shearing, or curing scab or other diseases. Behind this shed lay the *corrales,* or large cattle-yards— square enclosures, with high stone walls, used for shutting-up and branding the horned cattle. More to the right are placed enclosures of iron wire fencing, for cultivation or shutting-in the fine stock of Bheep introduced from Europe; whilst at a little distance appeared the nearest sheep stations: others, still farther away, so placed as to allow sufficient run or pasturage ground for each flock; the outside, or more distant ones, appearing like specks on the far-off horizon." ...

The Stations

"We soon arrived at one of the puestos: finding the flock feeding in the hollow near, under the care of the shepherd, and riding up to the hut — a well-built thatched house of two rooms — were sainted with genuine Irish welcome; found an increasing family of the *rael* breed, with the never-failing pig feeding about the door. There seemed, however, plenty and contentment. The husband gained about 35*l.* a year as shepherd, his sole employment being to take care of the flock placed under his charge. The wife told us, she made a nice thing by washing. They had their rations found— as much as they could eat. The sons and daughters, as they grew up, would early bring something to the general stock. As long as the country keeps at peace, there is no fear of want." ...

Investment of Capital

"We suppose the case of anyone starting with a capital of £1500. In such case, said he (the host), I should not venture to buy land; but should rent, for a term of years, what we call here a *suerte* — equal to about 5600 acres. This could be rented to-day for about £80 per annum, and would maintain easily 8000 sheep and 500 head of cattle. I have no doubt many will tell you that it will feed more; but it is, in my opinion, bad policy to overstock your land; for if a drought comes you will certainly suffer. If the land is first-rate, the longer your lease is the better. This done, I should invest my capital as follows: — ...

2400 sheep, about 10*s.* each		£1200
20 to 30 mares and horses		25
This stock requires two stations—		
One better-class, for residence ..	£100 ⎫	160
One smaller station	60 ⎭	
Furniture, a cart, and a few implements ..		40
		£1425

RETURNS.

	£
Original stock	2400
Increase, first year	800
,, second ,,	1000
,, third ,,	1400
,, fourth ,,	1400
,, fifth ,,	1800
	8800
Deduct sheep sold	1400
Stock at end of fifth year	7400
Original stock	2400
Increase	5000

	£		£
Receipt for wool, first year	180	Expenditure—first year	150
,, ,, second ,,	240	,, second ,,	180
,, ,, third ,,	320	,, third ,,	240
Sale of 1400 sheep ,, ,,	600	,, fourth ,,	240
Wool money, fourth ,,	230	,, fifth ,,	300
,, ,, fifth ,,	400		1110
Total receipt	2060	Rent of ground	400
,, expenditure	1510		1510
	550		
5000 sheep increase at 10s.	2500		
Houses, &c., at half-cost	100		
Profit in five years	3150		

Statement No. 2.

Capital £5000. Purchase of Land.

A suerte of land would cost 2000*l.*; stocking it with 3000 sheep, 1500*l.*; 600 head of cattle, 450*l.*; horses, 50*l.*; buildings and implements corresponding, 600*l.*; leaving a small surplus for contingencies. The increase on homed cattle is generally estimated at one-third on capital. The returns, therefore, in five years, may be roundly estimated as follows: —

		Stock of sheep.	Of cattle.
		3000	600
Increase, first year	.. ..	1000	200
,, second ,,	.. ..	1300	260
,, third ,,	.. ..	1700	360
,, fourth ,,	.. ..	1800	340
,, fifth ,,	.. ..	2000	400
		10,800	2160
	Sales	2800	800
		8000	1360
	Capital	3000	600
	Net increase	5000	760

RECEIPTS.	£	EXPENDITURE.	£
Wool money, first year ..	225	First year	300
,, second ,, ..	300	Second ,, ...	300
,, third ,, ..	520	Third ,, ...	350
,, fourth ,, ..	550	Fourth ,, ...	400
,, fifth ,, ..	450	Fifth ,, ...	450
1400 sheep sold	600		1800
1400 ,, ,, ...	600		
400 head of cattle	300		
400 ,, ,, ...	300		
	3845		
Deduct expenses ..	1800		
Surplus cash	2045		
5000 sheep	2500		
760 head of cattle ..	570		

Profit in 5 years £5115 on an outlay of £4600.

It is only fair to give the reverse of the picture from the same reliable authority. He says: —

"We spent two or three days in pleasant rides to other *puestos* (stations) of the Estancia; and visited some smaller establishments more recently founded by our countrymen: finding all well-contented and looking brightly on their future prospects. I am sure their success will be well merited, for it is not to be denied that the new beginner, with small means, must undergo some considerable hardships. Little do their comfortably-housed relatives at home know what a different picture the house presents here 1 And it is certainly very necessary for a man to have plenty of pluck before he settles as a sheep-farmer in these parts. It is all very well to tell you about a nice house, good dinner, a well-arranged establishment on a large scale, getting-up in the morning and finding your horses ready-saddled, and other things in the same pleasant strain — this is the end, and a very successful end; but to attain this you must have a beginning, and most generally with a limited capital. These reflections are forced upon me after my morning's visit to a young beginner, though I was glad to find he 'was not at all cast down by the deprivation he is passing through. He told me he started some two years since, renting land for two or three flocks. When he went to -work, there was not a building on the place; and whilst making his house he carted and carpentered with the others; the only difference, perhaps, was that he worked a good deal harder. They slept on the ground, with a few planks to cover them; they cooked by turns — beef and biscuit: a ready meal. At last he got his house up, and drove up his one flock; but with that his troubles seemed only beginning. By day, fearful lest he should lose part when any call took him out of their sight; at night, more so, from vermin or bad neighbours, or some sudden storm. Then came the wet days— out in all the storm, returning to the solitary hut cold and drenched, with no fire and nothing cooked, not a soul or welcome word to cheer or encourage. Perhaps you change and are getting a little warm, when you hear the flock going away, so you have again to start out. Again you get wet through, and perhaps find that your horses, as yet only half-settled, have cleared out for their former home. Then you begin with a few homed cattle — for you think it would be nice to have some, even if only to give you a little milk — but, like the horses, they will stray, and you have many weary rides in search of them, with an over-worked horse, in the heat of the sun — more trying even than the cold and rain. Besides all this, there is house drudgery, for a beginner is often his own cook and servant-of-all-work, and often you lie down as you get up; and the unswept floor encourages fleas and other insects, which increase more quickly than your sheep. These trials are the certain lot of all small beginners, but they go on with the hope of a bright future, and think of the next lambing season, and what increase they will get; and of the approaching clip, and what they will get for the wool: and build up a good many castles, I hope, for their sakes, on a good foundation. Certainly, however, with all its liberty, and the blue skies, and brilliant hopes, the starting is hard times."

The foregoing description of the country, with Statements of returns on capital invested, date probably from twenty years ago or more, but the *Estancia Accounts* can be compared with the following *bonâ fide* details, taken from a private letter from an English farmer in the Republic of Uruguay, and dated Aug. 13, 1881.

The writer says:

"It is hard to give an estimate of the working of an Estancia nowadays — everything is so completely changed. But one thing is certain, no man can do much, or anything, without fencing the 'camp' he occupies. The cost of fencing may be set down at about £40 or £50 per mile — that is, if the fencing is to keep in sheep as well as cattle.

"Rents of course vary according to situation, but to get land at anything like a low rent, one must go pretty well up to the frontiers of Brazil — the confines of civilisation. The working expenses of this Estancia — 2½ suertes [9] — 2400 cattle and 6000 sheep — amount to about 1000 dollars, £200 — per annum. This is of course inclusive of rent and taxes; and the sum I think could be gradually reduced to 900 dollars per annum.

"Last year's net results were close on 4500 dollars; and still, the 'camp' was not altogether occupied by our own stock. If it had been, there would have been quite 3000 dollars more of net profit.

"As to the result from sheep, I have had 'on halves' 2400 sheep, belonging to a friend ever since February 1874. I have remitted to him the following sums:

	$	£	s.	d.
1874	400·00	86	13	4
1875	474·60	98	19	5
1876	527·10	111	14	8
1877	447·65	98	3	2
1878	318·84	66	8	6
1879	463·68	100	16	3
1880	1092·54	234	7	10
in 7 years	3724·41	797	3	2

"His capital can be put down at 2400 dollars. He has received $3724 41c. and I have of course received the same amount. I have held sheep "on halves" from other people, since the year 1876, and the result has been just as good; so that the calculation must be made, not on one flock, but on the whole business. If my friend sells out at the end of 1881, he will receive more than the 2400 sheep or dollars, besides another year's wool money. The greater part of the seven years have been thoroughly bad ones for sheep, and particularly the year 1878. If I have attained such a result, there is no reason why anyone else should not do the same."

ANOTHER AND QUITE RECENT ESTIMATE (1882) IS HERE GIVEN OF 10 SUERTES OF GOOD CAMP, FENCED AND STOCKED

	$
10 suertes camp at $14,000 per suerte	140,000
15,000 head of cattle at $6 per head	90,000
20,000 sheep at $1 20c. per head	24,000
Fencing 22 running leagues, making— 6 paddocks, at $1500 per league	33,000
Houses, corrales, bath, etc.	10,000
Carts, tools, &c.	3,000
Horses and bullocks	1,500
	$301,500

CAPITAL INVESTED £64,000.
OUTLAY.

	$
Manager's salary	5,000
1 capataz at $30 per month	360
4 peones at $12 per month	576
1 house peon or cook at $25	300
6 shepherds and boys who look after fences and work at the estancia at $20	1,440
Cattle marking	200
Day peones (odd work)	1,500
Shearing expenses	2,000
Stores	1,500
Consumption of meat, pigs 100, sheep 960	1,118
Repairs and sundries	1,500
Taxes	1,000
	$16,494

INCOME.

	$
10 per cent. of Novillos to Saladero at $15	22,500
5 per cent. of cows to Saladero at $11	8,250
Nett increase of cattle, deducting sales 10 per cent. at $6	9,000
100 hides, animals killed	350
Wool from 26,000 sheep and lambs, 3 lb. at 35 rls. the arroba	10,920
Sale of 3000 wethers, at $1 80c.	5,400
Skins, 960 animals killed, 40c.	384
Nett value of increase of sheep	3,768
	$60,572
Deduct expenses	16,494
About 14½ per cent. on capital invested	$44,078

[1] The official value of 1*l*, is 4.70 dollars. The dollar is, therefore, worth rather more than 4s. 3d. In changing sterling money for the currency of the country, the ruling rate of Exchange has sometimes to be taken into account.
[2] Twenty years ago, and less, agriculture scarcely existed in the neighbouring provinces of Santa Fé and Buenos Aires, where, as in the Banda Oriental, the chief staples of production are hides and wool. In those days Buenos Aires imported wheat from Chile. This very year (1883), the exports of cereals from that city are expected to be nearly equal in value to those of wool. The small Italian farmers, or *chacreros,* in Buenos Aires and Santa Fé have accomplished what their fellow-countrymen as well as the Basques and the Canary Islanders will do in the Banda Oriental.
[3] A *fanega* is 225 lbs.
[4] A square *cuadra* is covered by 1.28 English acres. (See "Weights and Measures," page 167).
[5] Statistics taken from the Report published by the authority of the "Central Board of Immigration," Montevideo. 1878.
[6] Vivora de la Cruz. So called from marks like a cross on the creature's head. On the sugar-loaf mountain in a wild part of the coast near Maldonado, and in the mountains and stony lands of Las Minas there are rattle-snakes.
[7] Statistics for 1877.
[8] The flat roofs of the houses are called *azoteas.*
[9] See 'Money, Weights and Measures.'

General Statistics

Notwithstanding the crisis in 1875, three years afterwards, in 1878, land had not diminished in value. The average price of *pastoral land* in Uruguay, according to the tariff which serves as a guide to the Government in collecting the direct taxes on fixed property, was 3.77 dollars the hectare (2.47 English acres), or 6s. 5d. the acre.

Arable land was valued at 16.63 dollars the hectare — 28s. 7d. the acre.

It must be observed that the greater part of the pastoral lands can be converted into arable land.

In estimating the true value of landed property in the rural departments, the compiler of the official statistics, M. Vaillant, thought it right to add at least 50 per cent, to the prices quoted. According to the data afforded by the payment of direct taxes, the whole acreage of the Republic is thus divided: —

Pastoral lands	71·91 per cent.
Arable land in cultivation	1·24 ,,
Land occupied by houses and other buildings	0·11 ,,
Waste land, rivers, lakes, &c., and land without legitimate ownership	26·74 ,,

The value of the lands and houses of the Republic was estimated by M. Vaillant thus: —

Department of Montevideo	$91,659,977
Values not declared by the owners	6,000,000
	97,659,977
In the 12 departments[1]	81,958,837
50 per cent. added	40,979,418
Values not declared	16,000,000
	$236,598,232

The whole property of the Republic — lands, houses, live stock, and capital invested in commerce — he estimated at 75,531,975*l*., equal to 171*l*. for each inhabitant,

Don Federico Nin Reyes, the present Director of the Statistical Department, in his Report, dated June 12, 1882, calculates that in default of exact measurements, the fifteen departments of the territory of the Republic may be said to comprise an area of 7037.89 square leagues. In this area are 67 towns, containing together 20,000 urban and 25,000 rural habitations, each of a value exceeding $600, and therefore subject to the property tax.

This number of 45,000 house properties owned by an equal number of heads of families, each composed of five persons, demonstrates that 225,000 individuals, or one-half of the whole population, participate in the benefits of the possession of fixed property. The value of these properties is estimated at 360 millions of dollars— 76,500,000*l*.!— which is equal to M. Vaillant's estimate of the whole of the property of the Republic, and including commercial capital as well as live stock.

From the statistics which follow in regard to population or to the wealth of the Republic, it is therefore useless to attempt to form more than a general estimate, seeing that the authorities differ. Still, much is to be learned even from the different methods of valuation.

The pastoral establishments, says Señor Reyes, occupy some 14 millions of hectares of private landed property. Upon this space there exist 6,711,778 of cattle, 1,500,000 mares and horses, and 20 *millions of sheep*. About twenty *saladeros* and the same number of *graserías* — places for the making of tallow and grease — consume annually 550,000 oxen. The wool of the sheep is sorted and packed in seventy-five establishments called *barracas* into 43,980 bales of 1000 lbs. each, all of which, as well as other animal products, — hides, tallow, &c. — is exported.

The agricultural produce of the country does not as yet give a very large result. It occupies, nevertheless, 200,000 hectares of land, producing annually nearly one million *fanegas* of wheat, 400,000 of maize, a few seeds for the agricultural industry, and a quantity of poultry and vegetable and dairy produce suited to general consumption, which is valued at six millions of dollars annually.

The grinding of the wheat into flour employs 34 steam mills, 52 water mills and windmills, and about 200 smaller mills. These establishments could easily double their present production.

Rural properties in the Republic are burdened according to present calculations with mortgages to the extent of 10 millions of dollars.

The total of live stock in the Republic was formerly calculated in 1876 to be 19,191,273, divided thus: —

Cattle	6,092,488
Sheep	12,189,511
Mares	875,044
Mules, pigs, and goats	34,230
	19,191,273

In 1860 the total was 8,582,958, valued at $30,096,995.

In 16 years the increase was one million of cattle and ten millions of sheep, without counting cattle exported or consumed.

In 1878 the unofficial estimate of experienced landowners connected with the *Asociacion Rural* was

Cattle	7 millions
Sheep	14 "

In 1880 the official estimate of the total live stock in the Republic is again only 18,059,492 head, valued at $29,257,084.

The numbers and values are thus given: —

		Official values.
Cows	6,791,778	$23,771,223
Oxen	34,070	340,700
Mares	541,440	866,304
Horses	119,704	957,632
Mules	4,474	28,992
Sheep	10,568,026	3,160,812
Pigs	25,651	128,255
Goats	6,333	3,166
	18,059,492	$29,257,084

In taking the official number or values, it is necessary to add a very large percentage to find either the true number or true valuation. The amounts are taken from the declarations made by the proprietors, and the fiscal valuations are naturally under market prices.

At the ordinary valuations already given of cows, sheep, horses, &c., the 18,059,492 head of live stock would be worth $53,681,400.

Don Carlos Maria de Pena, one of the authors of the *Album de la Republica O. del Uruguay*, considers that in regard to cattle, in estimating the stock or wealth in cattle within the year we must add to the official number in 1880, which was

	7,491,466
For consumption in saladeros, and for food in the capital and on the estancias as well as for export across the frontier	1,143,988
Total head of cattle ..	8,635,454

This number at $6 per head equals $51,812,724.

Senor de Pena's detailed estimate is —

	Head of Cattle.
Consumption in Montevideo by the ships, saladeros and general population	272,640
Export of live animals	102,452
The Liebig factory at Fray·Bentos	146,005
Consumed on the estancias	400,000
Consumed in the saladeros on the River Uruguay, exclusive of the Liebig factory	222 891
	1,143,988

In regard to the total value of property in property. general in the Republic, it is stated in the Report of the Minister of Finance (1882) that from statistics given by the *Asociacion Rural* the increase in value of real property in the years 1880 and in 1881 may be estimated at 20 per cent, on rural properties and 10 per cent, on urban and suburban. According to the Direct Taxation statistics (Contribucion Directa) presented in that report, the declared value of

Rural properties in 1881 was	$121,012,414
Urban and suburban	94,709,440
Total ..	$215,721,854

This estimate includes live stock valued at 30 millions, and inclosures, wire fencing, &c., at 10 millions.

Following the example of M. Vaillant in the statistics given at the commencement of this chapter, at least 50 or 60 per cent, can be added to the total of 215 millions for values not declared and for low official valuations. Hence his estimate of the whole value of the property of the Republic at 75 millions sterling, includes commercial capital.

In a country where there is no systematic method as yet of taking a census, it is impossible to consider statistics of property or of population as anything more than arbitrary, and particularly in regard to nationalities.

The following table, showing the value of properties and the nationality of the owners, is for 1879, but the results are more or less the same as those given for 1881: —

Nationality of Proprietors.	Department of Monte Video. Proprietors.	Value.	The other 12 Departments. Proprietors.	Value.	Total. Proprietors.	Value.
		$		$		$
Native ..	2,940	40,831,785	12,450	48,780,592	15,354	89,612,387
Italian ..	2,346	20,287,431	2,553	6,267,556	4,899	26,556,987
Spanish	1,572	16,555,999	4,112	13,525,413	5,684	30,084,412
French ..	971	9,144,650	1,328	4,551,439	2,299	13,696,089
English ..	113	3,086,200	289	4,860,903	402	7,947,103
Brazilian	41	791,750	4,932	33,673,390	4,973	34,465,140
Portuguese	78	2,016,290	125	774,757	203	2,791,047
Argentine	123	3,065,747	465	1,910,017	588	4,975,764
German..	65	1,083,163	183	2,101,366	248	3,184,529
Swiss ..	31	146,000	196	277,097	227	423,097
African ..	10	28,600	..	..	10	28,600
Danish ..	4	75,500	..	..	4	75,500
North American	7	52,800	9	149,142	16	201,942
Austrian	7	37,300	1	5,300	8	40,800
Others ..	4	113,985	16	629,889	20	743,874
	8,276	97,319,200	26,659	117,505,061	34,935	214,824,261
Native ..	2,904	40,831,785	12,450	48,780,592	15,354	89,612,375
Foreign	5,372	56,487,415	14,209	68,734,469	19,581	125,211,887
	8,279	97,319,200	26,659	117,505,061	34,935	214,824,261

Any fixed quotations of present prices of land would be of little value, as the prices vary so much with the situation of the land, the time it has been stocked or under cultivation, the temporary demand, and other local considerations.

In the River Plate countries land varies from 1000*l.* to 6000*l.* the square league, and more according to the situation. Rents in former years have varied from 20*l.* to 80*l.*, and been even as high as 300*l.* or 400*l.* a league.

With the proviso that official valuations are very low and made for the purposes of direct taxation, the following values, taken from a projected law to come in force after revisal and discussion in the Legislature in the present year, 1883, will give a fair idea of the relative if not absolute values of agricultural and pastoral lands in different districts of the Republic.

PROPOSED GENERAL TARIFF OF LAND VALUES, 1883.

Department.	Agricultural, per square.[2]	Pastoral, per suerte.[2]
	$	$
Colonia	8	11,000
San José	8	11,000
Soriano	8	10,000
Paysandu and Rio Negro	8	10,000
Salto	8	10,000
From the bar of St. Lucia to the Salto in a zone of 2 leagues wide along the shores in these 6 departments, and with frontage to the rivers Plate and Uruguay with 2 leagues of length	..	15,000
Florida	8	10,000
Durazno	6	9,000

Departments.	Agricultural, per square.[2]	Pastoral, per suerte.[2]
	$	$
Cerro Largo	5	8,000
Tacuarembó	5	8,000
Maldonado and Rocha	6	8,000
Minas	6	8,000
Canelones between Pando and Toledo	20	..
" " Pando and Solis Chico	15	..
" in Canelon Grande	20	..
" between Piedras and Colorado	30	..
" Colorado and Canelon Grande	20	..
" between Canelon Grande and Tala	15	..
" in rest of the departments	10	..

Montevideo. In this department special valuations are made on urban and rural properties. The latter are not to be valued at less, in any case, than $50 the square, or *cuadra*.[2]

The valuations in this tariff show an increase varying from 6¼ to 36 2/3 per cent, on those of 1882.

The number of emigrants arriving in Montevideo during the years 1866 to 1871 inclusive was 103,682, being a yearly average in those six years of 17,280.

In 1872 there arrived	.. ..	15,516
,, 1873 ,,	,,	.. ..	24,339
,, 1874 ,,	,,	.. ..	13,757
,, 1875 ,,	,,	.. ..	5,298
,, 1876 ,,	,,	.. ..	5,570
,, 1877 ,,	,,	.. ..	6,168

Senor Don Aurelio Berro, ex-Minister of Finance, in his Report, dated February, 1880, says; —

"In regard to immigration, in the year just terminated (1879), 10,829 persons have arrived, against 6936 who have left the Republic, It is to be observed that one-third of the immigrants belong to the class of agricultural labourers."

On comparing the number of emigrants arriving in the nine years 1866 to 1874 with the comparatively few who arrived in the three following years, the falling off must not be absolutely ascribed to the commercial crisis. It was about the year 1866 that transatlantic steam navigation from the Mediterranean began to assume its present proportions; and in the south of Europe there was something like a mania for emigration. The emigration from Italy in the years 1866, 1867, and 1868 formed nearly one half of the whole emigration to Montevideo. It included a vast number of Neapolitans of a low class, who earned, in the city and its environs, but a few dollars, and have returned to their own country. The tide of emigration is now again turning to Montevideo, and it will be quite as advantageous if fewer arrive than in those years, should the immigrants he of a better class, or more adapted to rural pursuits and permanent settlement.

In the ten years 1867 to 1876, 154,223 passengers have arrived in the port of Montevideo, Of these 16,367 have applied to the *Central Board of Immigration;* 1112 have been housed by the Board; and 15,525 have received employment through the aid of the Board. 41,214 have received employment direct, in the city or departments. Of those who have presented themselves to the Board of Immigration, 33.54 per cent, were Spaniards; 33.13 per cent. Italians; 16.48 per cent. French; 4.51 per cent. English; 12.34 per cent, various.

Señor Lucio Rodriguez, Secretary of the Central Board of Immigration, calculates that in 12 years (1867-1878) Uruguay received 169,778 immigrants, of whom only 1335 were lodged at the expense of the Board.

The great falling off in the immigration during the years 1873 to 1877 has continued more or less to the period included in the latest statistics (1882). Now that the country is reviving, there is every hope that the flow of emigration from Europe will return to the Republic of Uruguay, as it has done to the neighbouring Republic, where, after a comparative lull, the number of immigrants by the latest accounts has reached 10,000 monthly.

The Government of Uruguay has established Board of a "Board" or "Central Commission of Immigration." The Government has no agents in Europe, and has made no attempts to influence emigration until quite lately, when it drew the attention of its consuls in Europe to the subject.

The "Central Commission" was formed simply with the object of giving advice to immigrants on their arrival in the country, helping them to obtain employment, and, in exceptional cases, affording pecuniary assistance.

The Commission is aided in its duties by the authorities and officials of the port on the arrival of the emigrant vessels.

It has also obtained the co-operation of the proprietors of the *Villa Colon* — an important rural establishment situated six miles from the capital — where newly-arrived immigrants who are able and willing to work are provided with hoard and lodging gratis, until they find permanent and remunerative employment.

In November 1879 an Asylum for Immigrants was established, which holds 1000 persons, and contains 24 rooms for families, offices, &c. Up to January 1880, $1782 have been expended in ten months, and shelter has been provided for 1270 individuals. The greater portion of these were Italians, and there were also a few French, Germans, and Swiss. These were all placed ultimately in the "Swiss" and "Cosmopolitan" agricultural colonies. The Government facilitated their transport by steamer and railway. In consequence of the circular issued by the Government to the European consuls in respect to emigration, some 20 families, in all 131 persons, arrived in April 1880. The Government was not well prepared for their arrival, but it did all that was possible, and advanced to them $5032, repayable in five years, and found them employment in the agricultural colonies.

The Report of the Ministry of Finance (1882) says: — "It is generally supposed that immigration increases consumption, and by its additional labour increases production. Truly, it is well to consider the point, since the increase of population in a fertile and progressive country like this Republic is one of the fundamental elements of its advance. But it is desirable that the immigration should be voluntary, spontaneous, and not fomented by contracting agents abroad, who as a rule promise more than they can perform, and the ultimate benefit is slight either to the colonist or to the country to which he emigrates. The voluntary emigrant will elect the country which is progressive, the climate that is most healthy, and the place where the best security is offered to his labour, as well as to the capital he may possess. Moreover, it is well to bear in mind that, in order that the current of immigration shall be a reality as in the United States or in the Argentine Republic, it is necessary that a country shall offer to the immigrant the land he has to cultivate and make productive, and on such easy conditions that the results of his labour shall at the outset secure him a fair living. It is difficult to imagine that agriculturists and their families who may be more or less well off in their own countries will transfer themselves to this Republic without guarantee that they will find lands suited to their labour and calling; and at present in the Republic there is no practical, useful, and far-seeing legislation with the object of apportioning the public lands and dividing properties without prejudice to the actual possessors and raising serious questions in the future."

This very frank statement on the part of the then Minister of Finance, Senor Don Juan L. Cuestas, can only be understood as indicating his desire to urge on the attention of the Government the necessity which exists for something analogous to a "homestead law" in the Republic for the better encouragement of immigration.

Apart from special legislation in regard to that question, the present mode of acquiring by purchase and of transferring land in the Republic of Uruguay as in other River Plate countries, is simple and inexpensive. The instrument of transfer drawn up by the lawyer, and containing a detailed description of the land sold and its boundaries, is copied by the duly appointed notary in a register; and the copy is signed by the seller and purchaser, at the office of the Registrar. Formerly, the purchase-money was paid there and then, in the presence of the Registrar; but it is now usually understood that when the document is signed the transaction has been completed, either by cash payment or sufficient security. A copy of the deed of transfer, duly certified by the public notary, can be procured at any time for a small fee. The register — with the mortgages (if any) which are in the first instance or subsequently charged on the property — are open to public inspection.

There are no means of tying up property by devices similar to the English laws of settlement and entail. Property is, as elsewhere, divided into fixed and movable property; but there is not, as in England, any legal and artificial distinction between real and personal estate. The interests of children and minors are, however, protected by a specially appointed judge, styled a *Juez de Menores*.

Lands purchased from the State are subject to the usual conditions, if they are paid for by instalments, or by a certain amount of rental for a specified period. The land, in these cases, must be stocked and utilised to a limited extent, according to the terms of agreement generally exacted in the sale of State lands.

Mr. Monson, the British Minister, in his last report says: — "With regard to the administration of justice, the old Spanish procedure is still generally in use, and the law's delays, proverbial in every country, are here exaggerated to an insupportably wearisome extent. Prisoners arrested on criminal charges have been known to remain for years in confinement before they are brought to trial; while civil causes are prolonged as interminably and expensively as the most enthusiastic admirer of our own old Chancery practice could possibly desire. That the profession of the law in this country must be a lucrative one appears to be proved by the number of practitioners; and the cause list published in the daily papers falls not very far short of its prototype in the London journals. But it must not be supposed that in what has just been said there is any intention of imputing unfairness or partiality to the tribunals. On the contrary, the foreigner is at least as well treated and as certain of obtaining justice as the native; and more than one important judicial appointment is held by a man of foreign origin. The country magistrate, 'Juez de Paz,' is not perhaps always a legal luminary, but he is no worse than many a member of the great unpaid, to whose judicial sagacity our own rural population is content to submit its plaints."

The immigrants most needed in the Republic are agricultural labourers and female servants. These can be sure of finding employment Steady young men of good constitutions and accustomed to outdoor country life, can earn at the sheep farms from 3*l.* to 4*l.* a month, with board and lodging; and after a short time usually get a flock of sheep with a third of the profits: ultimately they become independent farmers.

The language of the country is Spanish; but in the capital, and in some parts of the rural departments, there are a great many English residents. In the neighbourhood of the capital French and Italian are general. Unmarried English women — of good conduct and some experience in housekeeping — are, notwithstanding their ignorance of Spanish, much in request in native families. They earn from 2*l.* to 3*l.* a month, with all found. Married couples, without families, are also in demand. The husband may act as herdsman, sheep-keeper, farm labourer, or gardener, and the wife can be employed as cook, or in other domestic duty. Their joint wages may be calculated at 70*l.* per annum, with board and lodging.

Some of the wealthiest landed proprietors now in the River Plate were either themselves originally English, Irish, or Scotch settlers, who have gradually acquired landed property, or they are the sons or grandsons of such men. The successful foreign merchant often retires after a certain number of years to his own country, and takes his family with him; but the sheep-feeder and land-owner — emanating from a different class, and with no pleasing reminiscences of his own country — remains to found a family and name in the land of his adoption. Some years ago, the sheep-feeding districts of the River Plate were overrun by young Englishmen of education and good connections. As a rule they did not succeed, and in the few instances to the contrary they returned, like the merchants, to their own country when they had the opportunity.

According to the celebrated traveller Felix de Azara, the Banda Oriental contained, in 1796, 30,685 inhabitants; including 15,245 in the City of Montevideo. One half of the latter lived outside the walls and at some distance. In 1813 the population of the city was calculated at 16,000. In 1829 — the epoch of the declaration of independence — the whole Republic contained 74,000 inhabitants. In 1852 — after the war and long siege of the capital by General Oribe — the Republic contained a population of 131,969. Eight years after, in 1860, the number of the population rose to 221,300: an increase of 89,331. In 1873, the population was estimated at 450,000: and in 1878 at was estimated at a little over 438,000; and according to the following table, taken from the government report of 1882, that number seems to be still adhered to in the official statistics, which give the following enumeration: —

DISPERSION OF THE POPULATION IN REGARD TO NATIONALITY IN THE 15 DEPARTMENTS.

Departments.	Natives.	Spanish.	Italians.	French.	Brazilian.	Argentines.	English.	German.	Other Nations.	Total.
Canelones	37,155	4,500	4,186	1,360	1,215	2,198	262	288	1,167	52,331
Colonia	17,800	1,960	2,623	938	56	1,552	220	314	1,588	27,051
Soriano	13,543	1,554	2,015	768	162	1,546	152	285	191	20,216
San José	20,542	3,837	1,741	862	88	279	165	80	242	27,776
Maldonado and Rocha	21,924	1,375	988	131	1,288	85	..	..	245	26,036
Florida	18,019	1,076	938	291	247	120	83	27	87	20,888
Paysandu and Rio Negro	20,212	2,922	3,080	884	4,345	1,427	170	187	758	33,985
Salto	15,216	1,016	1,312	394	6,029	1,505	112	75	282	25,941
Cerro Largo	16,815	2,104	1,597	636	1,493	1,028	122	134	546	24,475
Durazno	11,360	1,376	1,280	416	371	672	80	88	357	16,000
Tacuarembó	20,569	2,672	2,484	807	2,201	1,304	155	171	692	31,055
Minas	18,368	888	459	168	863	80	21	14	130	20,991
In departments	231,523	25,280	22,703	7,655	18,358	11,796	1,482	1,663	6,285	326,745
In department of Montevideo	66,550	14,500	13,600	6,720	1,820	3,750	1,290	462	2,858	111,500
Total	298,023	39,780	36,303	14,375	20,178	15,546	2,772	2,125	9,143	438,245

Departments.	Chief Towns.	Population.
Rocha and Maldonado	Rocha and Maldonado	26,036
Canelones	Guadalupe	52,331
Montevideo	Montevideo	111,500
San José	San José	27,776
Colonia	Colonia	27,051
Soriano	Mercedes	20,216
Rio Negro	Constitucion	12,833
Paysandu	Paysandu	21,152
Salto	Salto	25,941
Tacuarembó	San Fructuoso	31,055
Cerro Largo	Melo	24,475
Entre Yi y Rio Negro	Durazno	16,000
Florida	Florida	20,888
Minas	Minas	20,991
	Total	438,245

The natives form 68.33 per cent, of the whole population of the Republic, 69 '65 per cent, in the department of Montevideo; and 70 to 86 per cent, in the other fourteen departments; but, as already observed, this proportion includes the children of foreign residents. In the fifteen departments.

The Spaniards form	8·66 per cent.
„ Italians „	8·31 „
„ Brazilians „	4·62 „
„ Argentines „	3·56 „
„ French „	3·29 „
„ English „	0·63 „
„ Germans „	0·48 „
Other nations	2·12 „

The proportion of foreigners in the Republic is 31.67. In the department of Montevideo it is 40.35; and in the fourteen rural departments, 29-14.

The total number of British subjects is 2772; of whom 1290 are in the metropolitan department of Montevideo, and 1482 in the rural departments.

The statistics given above are evidently more or less the same as those compiled by Don Adolfo Vaillant in 1877. Later estimates compiled from police and educational statistics demonstrate that if, allowing for errors, the population of the Republic at the highest estimate exceeds 440,000, it is certainly under 460,000.

The density of the population in the several departments is estimated as follows: —

Departments of	Montevideo,	per kilomètre	166	inhabitants.
"	Canelones,	"	8·42	"
"	Colonia,	"	4·11	"
"	Soriano,	"	2·77	"
"	San José, Florida, Paysandu, Maldonado Salto, Cerro Largo, Minas, and Durazno, per kilomètre		1·16	
"	Tacuarembó,	"	0·72	"

The average density of the population in the whole territory of the Republic is 2.35 per square kilometre. In the Argentine Republic the density is 1.28; but in the metropolitan province of Buenos Aires it is 3.84. In Chile — a mining and agricultural country — the density of the population is 6.02.

In Belgium, which is not as large as the single department of Tacuarembó in the Republic of Uruguay, the density of the population in 1878 — the period at which these comparisons were made — was 165 inhabitants per square kilometre.

Were the territory of the Republic as thickly populated as the department of Canelones, with a density of eleven inhabitants per square kilometre, the whole population would amount to 1,678,275.

Were all the departments populated like that of Montevideo, Uruguay would contain 31,000,000 of inhabitants.

In the years 1876, 1877, and 1878 the proportion of legitimate and illegitimate children baptised, was in the department of

	Legitimate.	Illegitimate.
Montevideo	94·80	5·20
In the rural departments	74·08	25·92
In the whole Republic	79·16	20·84

In tables of mortality and hygienic data the statistics of the country are defective; and what exist relate principally to the metropolitan department

To administer to the wants of the rural population who sustain the activity of other industries, there are in the Republic 300 factories of various kinds; 257 mercantile houses; 153 barracas or deposits; 33 wholesale dealers: 3 banks of issue, deposit and discount; 40 exchange offices; 29 auctioneers; 13 depôts of agricultural machinery; 35 ironmongers; 35 clothiers; 426 establishments of collectors of produce (*acopiadores*); 42 furniture shops; 33 hatters; 160 tailors; 412 shoemakers; 849 grocery stores; 2673 small retail stores; 163 hotels, inns, and wine-cellars; 412

drapers' shops; and 400 different establishments of carpenters, lithographers, watchmakers, and other trades. It is calculated there are more than 1000 professional men.

[1] Two new departments, *Rocha* and *Rio Negro,* were established by a law passed in July, 1880, making, with the department of Montevideo, 15 in all.
[2] See table of "Moneys, Weights, and Measures,".

Trade and Commerce

Exports and Imports

The official value of the special commerce of Uruguay is given by Senor Vaillant, for the year 1878, thus:—

Imports	$15,927,974
Exports	17,492,159
Total	$33,420,133

divided between the different nations as follows: —

	Imports.	Exports.
England	$4,884,878	$4,398,790
France	2,622,997	3,147,504
Brazil	1,955,254	4,244,778
United States and Canada	982,175	1,095,370
Spain	1,368,140	38,101
Germany	808,935	74,334
Italy	867,343	286,524
Belgium	379,622	1,775,582
Other Countries	2,058,630	2,431,176
	$15,927,974	$17,492,159
		15,927,974
	Total	$33,420,133

The word *special* is employed to separate the absolute trade and consumption of the Republic from the *transit trade* which passes through Montevideo to and from Brazil, Buenos Aires, and the Ports of the Paraná. Comparing the Customs Returns made in England, France, &c., of goods exported to Uruguay, it was found in former years that they amounted sometimes to upwards of 64 per cent, more than the returns made of the corresponding imports in Montevideo. Part of this discrepancy was attributed to contraband trade, and part to the low tariff of valuation at the Montevidean Custom House; but the main reason was that in the statistics of Uruguay no notice was taken of the goods or produce imported and re-shipped to Buenos Aires, &c., or to Europe. Since 1877 rectifications have been made; and it is possible that the discrepancies in regard to the transit trade may have been exaggerated; but from the latest official reports (1882) it does not appear that the question is yet solved. In respect to the official value of produce such as wool and hides in transit through Montevideo from Brazil and the Argentine Republic, the amount seems to have been in 1881, $1,176,447; the real value, the collector of customs places at $1,500,000. As to the more important question of articles of commerce in general imported from Europe, and re-shipped to Buenos Aires or other neighbouring ports, there do not appear to be any official data.

In regard to discrepancies between the British Board of Trade Returns and the official statistics of the Republic, the difference is generally in the exports from Uruguay. For example, in the year 1878 —

	Uruguay Statistics.	Board of Trade.
The exports to Great Britain were ..	£935,912	£644,066
The imports from „ „ ..	1,039,335	1,035,145
	£1,975,247	£1,679,211

This difference is accounted for by vessels clearing for British ports and calling for orders. There is also the question of freight; and there may be other minor causes of variation.

The imports from Great Britain, in 1878, amount to about a third of the whole import trade; and the exports to Great Britain amount to about one-fourth of the exports oi Uruguay. The whole trade with Great Britain amounts to about three-elevenths of the total exports and imports of the country; whereas the trade with France amounts to less than two elevenths.

But turning to other statistics, and for 1877, we find that — taking the Customs Returns in England and France of exports to Uruguay— each inhabitant of the latter country consumes or *negotiates,* to the value of 20*l.* 17*s.*, of French goods, and 17*l.* 18*s.* of English goods. That is to say, the *special* trade with Uruguay is in favour of Great Britain, but the special and *transit trade* combined show a balance in favour of France. Something in this question depends on the method of valuing articles exported in England and in France,

The returns of exports and imports, according to the trade with each nation, are confessedly in round numbers. An *ad valorem* valuation is in itself seldom exact in an estimate, for example, of cheap English goods compared with the fancy articles of French manufacture. Again, in estimating the exports to Brazil, it would be impossible — without a *cordon* of Customs officers on the frontier — to determine what quantities of live cattle were driven over from the northern departments of Uruguay into Brazil without paying duties at all.

The total imports and exports of the Republic, in 1864, amounted to 14,718,873 dollars — the lowest figures during the fourteen years, 1862-1877 inclusive. In 1873, they rose to 37,377,218 dollars. In 1875 they fell to about 25 millions; and rose again, in 1877, to 28,824,658 dollars.

Comparing the trade statistics for the years 1840-42 with those of 1872-73, it appears that the exports of salted and dry hides — representing the principal industry of the country — remained the same after an interval of 30 years. The value of the hides, however, increased.

The exports of wool, in 1872-73, amounted to sixteen times the quantity exported in 1840-42. The exports of tallow and grease increased to four times the quantity; and of horse-hair to three times. The exports of jerked beef showed only a slight increase. A email manufactured article of export, *candles* — never very important, ceased altogether in 1872. The export of ostrich feathers rose from 1010 kilos to 23,962 kilos and the prices rose from 80 cents to 1.50 and 2.50 dollars per lb.

The chief articles of export from Uruguay to the United Kingdom are hides, tallow, and wool.

The imports of Uruguay from Great Britain consist principally of manufactured cotton and woollen goods.

In the prosperous year, 1874, the Exports to the United Kingdom,

Were valued at	£1,437,288
The imports, at	1,304,156
	£2,741,444

The difference in the total trade between the two countries, in 1878 compared with 1874, shows a decrease of 766,187*l*.: accounted for by the recent crisis and depression in the bulk of trade as well as in prices. [1]

The customs valuations in the Returns of exports and imports are supposed to be quite 30 per cent, under the real value.

In the years 1873-75, the amount of the total imports and exports gave an average of 72.06 dollars for each inhabitant of Uruguay. In the Argentine Republic, the average was 47.55; and in Chile 30.53, The consuming and productive powers of Uruguay are Ho doubt very great in proportion to the population, and indicate — in the Metropolitan Department of Montevideo at all events — a very high standard of comfort and even of luxury. At the present date, from the official statistics of 1882 it appears that the relative producing and consuming powers of the three republics are —

	Population.			Per Inhabitant.
Argentine Republic	2,400,000	exports and imports	$41·90
Chile	2,100,000	"	"	38·95
Uruguay	450,000	"	"	87·17

From these figures it would result that the inhabitants of Uruguay consume nearly 140 per cent more than the inhabitants of the Argentine Republic, and 200 per cent, more than those of Chile; and produce 80 per cent, more than the Argentines, and 75 per cent, more than the Chilians. But to arrive at anything like the truth, in regard to the commonly given inferences from statistical data, there are sometimes collateral questions to consider, not always attended to. For example, in this case, Chile in particular, and the Argentine Republic in a less degree, are agricultural countries. The mere values of exports and imports are not a sufficient test of the relative consuming or producing powers of different nations. All that a nation *consumes of its own produce,* would absolutely tell against it, in a bald valuation of exports and imports. The more it consumed of its own produce, the less it would export; and to a certain extent, but not in the same proportion, the less it would have occasion to import. The Collector of Customs in his Report (1881) alludes to this question, and points out that *new industries* have appeared, and especially in articles of clothing. But if as he states the new industries, which have been fostered by high duties, have diminished imports, the case is not the same as with the natural industries of the country. The extra cost of the articles of clothing will have to be paid for by abstention, or as a tax on the consumer in one way or another. The Collector on the other hand deplores the fact that a pastoral country like Uruguay should import *butter* and *cheese,* at an additional cost of at least 40 per cent., including freight, charges, and duties. This is probably a question of scarcity of labour, and ultimately of immigration; but in this case the complaint is just, and imports of that nature might diminish with advantage.

The value of the *exports* in 1881 was over 20 millions of dollars; and allowing for a liberal Customs valuation in favour of the exporters, the amount may safely be calculated at 25 millions, or over 5,000,000*l*. The *imports* amounted to $17,108,488, or $2,570,380 less than in 1880, equal to 12 per cent, reduction. The *imports* in late years have not reached the figures, somewhat exceptional, of 1872 and 1873, but they show a steady general increase, and for some time the imports exceeded the exports; but not on that account was there any diminution in commercial activity.

In the period of six years from 1870 to 1875 the imports amounted to

	$99,415,830
From 1876 to 1881	97,121,475
Diminution	$2,294,364

In the same period the exports were: —

1870 to 1875	$85,842,972
1876 to 1881	103,746,238
Increase	$17,903,266

The average value of the annual *imports* in the twelve years 1870 to 1881, inclusive, is $16,378,101, and of the exports, $15,799,184

The exports and imports for 1881, the values of which have been already given, show therefore a very large increase on the annual average during the past twelve years.

The following Tables show the question of exports and imports for the last five years more in detail.

TOTAL EXPORTS AND IMPORTS, 1877 TO 1881, INCLUSIVE.

	Imports.		Exports.		Totals of Imports and Exports.	
	Dollars.	Sterling.	Dollars.	Sterling.	Dollars.	Sterling.
	$	£	$	£	$	£
1877	15,045,846	3,201,243	15,899,406	3,382,852	30,945,252	6,584,095
1878	15,927,974	3,338,930	17,492,159	3,721,736	33,420,133	7,060,666
1879	15,919,903	3,393,597	16,645,961	3,541,694	32,565,864	6,935,291
1880	19,478,868	4,144,410	19,752,201	4,202,596	39,231,069	8,347,006
1881	17,918,884	3,812,529	20,229,512	4,304,152	38,148,396	8,116,681

Exports and Imports, 1881.

Countries.	Imports.	Exports.	Totals.
	$	$	$
Great Britain	5,381,054	3,191,959	8,573,013
France	2,906,949	4,069,847	6,976,796
Brazil	2,193,492	3,519,639	5,713,131
United States	1,269,778	3,867,491	5,137,272
Spain	1,894,463	265,966	2,160,429
Germany	1,181,145	69,826	1,250,971
Italy	1,032,194	583,083	1,615,277
Belgium	453,764	1,875,730	2,329,494
Argentine Republic	464,018	1,040,302	1,504,320
Cuba	155,791	689,302	845,093
Switzerland	32,580	..	32,580
Chile	134,888	118,107	252,995
Holland	144,227	..	144,227
India, China, and Japan	84,965	200	85,165
Peru	13,156	297	13,453
Paraguay	114,480	5,212	119,692
Portugal	43,375	171,191	214,566
Sweden and Norway	8,268	..	8,268
Austria-Hungary	586	..	586
Russia and Denmark	1,190	..	1,190
W. Indies, Mauritius, and Réunion	5,609	28,729	34,338
Santa Cruz and Teneriffe	1,844	31,400	33,244
Falkland Islands	..	1,184	1,184
Cape of Good Hope	..	126,668	126,668
Other countries	401,068	573,376	974,444
Total in 1881	$17,918,884	20,229,502	38,148,396
Specie	1,889,905	2,468,114	4,358,019

Independently of the staple exports, such as wool, hides, and tallow, and the importation of manufactured goods, the exports and imports of provisions have a special interest in the trade of Montevideo. The provision trade is a characteristic of the port, that from its geographical position is largely indebted to a transit trade, a large part of which consists of liquors, sugar, rice, tobacco, oil, cereals, and other articles of general consumption, that pass through Montevideo to the ports on both sides of the River Plate and the River Uruguay, as well as to ports of Brazil and Paraguay in the interior regions watered by the, Uruguay and Paraná. The provision trade is also a fair test of the well-being of the population of the Republic itself, and is intimately connected, as a question of exports, with the rising agricultural industries of the country.

According to the *Revista Mercantil* of 1883, the falling off already noticed in the general imports in 1882, compared with 1881, is of more importance than appears from the mere figures, which show only a trifling deficit.

The value of the imported articles included under the head of *provisions* and *groceries,* which in Montevideo technically comprise a few articles that are not exactly eatables and drinkables, was, in 1881, $8,648,000. In 1882 the value of the same description of imports was $8,514,000. These values are calculated on prices in bond. The difference in favour of the year 1881 is $134,000. But in 1881 there were many articles, such as figs, olives, oil, soap, macaroni, liquors, &c., from Spain, France, Naples, Genoa, Brazil, and the Argentine Republic, that were not included in the estimate for 1881, as the returns had not been made in time for the publication of the documents given by the *Revista Mercantil*. These articles figure in the estimate for 1882, and increased the imports in that year, compared with the preceding, by $752,000. Moreover the prices in 1881 were much higher — at least 5 per cent. — so that the absolute deficit in 1882 is $1,274,000.

This result would be disheartening, were it not that irregularities in regard to stocks and prices of provisions arise from a very simple cause. The provision trade in Montevideo is in the hands of a few firms, generally speaking of good repute, but old-fashioned in their methods. They have been accustomed to receive their importations at certain periods corresponding with the fall in prices in the producing countries, and always in sailing vessels. The varying requirements of the home market have not been considered, so that generally speaking in the provision trade it is either a feast or a famine. The present substitution of steamers for sailing vessels is rapidly changing the whole business, equalising, and perhaps lowering, prices, and regulating supplies. This question is interesting, as a minute illustration of great changes in commerce throughout the world, due to altered conditions, irrespective of temporary causes and of the relative values of the currency and of gold.

The export of cereals, flour, fruits, hay, and oleaginous products, to Brazil, the West Indies, the Cape of Good Hope, and to Europe, is destined before long to be of some importance to the Republic. At present the exports of agricultural produce are not of much value; and at least three-fourths of the flour, for instance, exported from Montevideo in 1882, were in transit from Chile. But agriculture in general, and new agricultural industries, such as wines, honey, beer, spirits, silk, oils, and dairy produce, are fast emerging from the state of mere experiment, due to wealthy and enterprising individuals. The Italian and the Basque cultivators are modernising the barbarous methods employed by the descendants of the Canary Islanders, and are extending their operations beyond the hitherto strictly agricultural departments of Montevideo and Canelones, and are following the rivers and lines of railway into the departments of San José, Colonia, Florida, Soriano, Rio Negro, and Maldonado. The newest agricultural implements by the first English and American makers are to be found in most parts of the country. The capital recently invested in agricultural machinery cannot be much less than a million of dollars.

These implements are not necessarily in the hands of small cultivators, but their presence in a district will raise the ambition and improve the methods of labour. As for the agriculturist on a very small scale, it is calculated that a family can establish themselves on a patch of land of 30 or 40 acres, and provide themselves with a house, to working oxen, a milch cow, two carts, and the necessary implements, at a cost of under 50*l*. Their expenditure, including rent, and allowing for ten per cent, interest, would within the first year be about 60*l*. With fair luck, the produce of the land should yield them a net profit of 18*l*. or 20*l*. to add to their capital. In the neighbourhood of Montevideo the small cultivators are for the most part the owners of the soil, on which they raise wheat, [maize, potatoes, and *alfalfa* - lucern.

[1] The total exports and imports from Uruguay to all countries amounted in 1879 to £6,036,289; showing a slight decrease compared with 1878.

Public Revenue

History of the Public Debt

In the year 1827 the budget of the Banda Oriental amounted only to $138,300, equal in the money of the present day to $110,640, or 23,508*l*. In 1829 it rose to $729,928. The public finances at that time were in course of organisation; and it is not strange that, three years later, in 1832, owing to an improved system and greater economy, the amount should have fallen to $492,309, apportioned, thus:—

Government Department and Foreign Affairs	$182,778
War and Marine	306,425
Financial Department	86,184
	$575,387
Houses of Legislature and other expenses	40,000
Old money	$615,387
Present money	$492,309

In 1835 the budget rose to $767,729 (old money), but in that year there was a surplus over the actual expenditure of $271,626.

In 1829 the public debt amounted to $153,000. In 1830 it rose to $430,000. Treasury notes were issued for its redemption, and in December, 1831, it was reduced to $107,000.

But during the rule of the Provisional Government under General Rondeau, in 1830, financial complications had already appeared.

On the 15th February, 1834, the public debt had risen to $879,000, and in February, 1835, the Commission appointed to report on the finances of the State announced a deficit of "the enormous sum," as they called it, of $1,474,625. The debt about that date had risen to $2,081,000, and the fruitful source of difficulties was in the war department, which in those days consumed 50 per cent, of the receipts of the State. Moreover, at more or less the same period, some of the loans of the Government were contracted at rates varying from 18 to 30 per cent, per annum.

In 1836 the total receipts were calculated at $917,000. Of this sum, $74,000 were from Custom duties on imports. The receipts from all sources in that year very much exceeded the estimates. The financial position of the country seemed favourable, and efforts were made to redeem a portion of the public debt. From 1832 to 1836 the receipts had not much varied in amount, but from 1836 to 1842 they increased 300 per cent. Unhappily the obligations and expenditure had begun to increase at a still higher rate. In 1840 the receipts were $3,029,385 (old money), but the cash deficit and public debt amounted to $5,128,378 and 7 rials, as officially stated, with the remark that "the country was at the *brink of an abyss.*"

Foreign complications, and particularly with the Argentine Confederation, soon began to magnify the "supplementary" and "extraordinary" estimates of the war department; and finally came the *Guerra Grande*, or "great war," when the country was invaded by General Oribe, by orders of the dictator of the Argentine Confederation, General Don Manuel Rosas.

The ordinary resources of revenue, export and import duties, were reduced, and some of them disappeared. Tributes, forced loans, and similar devices served as the financial basis of the organisation of the defence of the besieged city of Montevideo, The interest of money in private transactions at that period was at the rates of 40, 50, 80, and even 100 per cent per annum! The public properties were sold at ruinous prices. The Customs revenue in 1844 and 1845 was farmed, and produced very little — something over $200,000 in each year.

After the peace in 1851, the ordinary expenditure of the year was placed at $2,000,000. During the years 1852 and 1853 the country again revived. The stock of cattle began to increase, and commerce returned to its old channels. Notwithstanding internal political dissensions which quickly declared themselves, the revenue of the country in 1854 was $2,611,000, and in 1869 it had increased to six-fold the amount raised in 1829.

The public debt increased likewise, and its service was at the same time gradually organised. The consolidation of the debt due to private persons for State exactions took place in 1854. In 1857 the conversion was arranged of the debt due for compensations of losses during the great war. In 1859 a contract was made with Baron Maud for the conversion of the consolidated debts, and the creation of a public funded debt, the operation commencing with $80,000,000. The creditors, represented by the Maud Bank, ceded 95 per cent, of the nominal value of the consolidated bonds, and the interest to July 1, 1859. The rate of interest on this funded debt was fixed at 6 per cent., with 1 per cent, sinking fund; the redemption to be by tender until the bonds were at par, when it would take place by drawing.

The whole debt of the State in August, 1857, was calculated at $104,639,242 (old money). In 1863 an arrangement was proposed with Mauá and Co. for the funding of the *Internal Debt*, amounting to $2,500,000; and in 1864 the *Internal Debt* was converted into an *External National Debt* to the amount of one million sterling, issued by Baron Maua in London; interest 6 per cent., and 1 per cent, sinking fund.

This was the first step taken by the Republic towards contracting a foreign debt.

Once initiated, and with some difficulty, the system was very soon pursued on a larger scale. *The Uruguay Loan,* to the amount of $16,450,000, was negotiated in London in 1871. The history of that loan belongs to recent times.

The revenue of the Republic of Uruguay is derived principally from the Customs dues. A part is derived from direct taxation on land and houses, and from stamps, stamped paper, and licenses to business houses, shops, &c.

The Custom Revenues, in 1878, were $5,900,000
„   „   1879, „   4,900,300

But during the latter part of the year 1879 the import duties were reduced 50 per cent. In allusion to this reduced tariff, which was quickly abandoned, the Report of the Minister of Finance for the year 1881 says: — "The importing trade alone benefited by the reduction of duties. The consumer derived no perceptible advantage. Moreover, the traders had no confidence in the measure, as they did not consider it serious or permanent, and thus kept up their old prices. The Treasury, therefore, lost the difference in the Customs duties, whilst the consumer neither consumed more goods nor more cheaply."

The Minister in his report acknowledges the necessity of faithfully maintaining the credit of the Republic, so that foreign capitalists may have no doubt as to the desire and ability to fulfil the contracts she may have entered into. The administration of the public funds has of late years visibly improved, and efforts are being made to perfect the system of levying Customs dues, upon which the principal portion of the national revenue depends. As the Minister observes, there are so many conflicting interests to be considered, it is no easy matter to solve at once the problems that arise in the administration of the Customs. Above all it is necessary that the Customs duties should be uniform; and yet, as the Report states, it was not very long ago that, in the endeavour to compete with the Brazilian custom-houses, lower duties were levied on the frontier than in other parts of the Republic. The consequence was that a merchant in Paysandú would purchase his goods in Salto, where the duties were lower; and such anomalies must occur when general principles of justice and common sense are abandoned in favour of some temporary device in the shape of differential duties. Much has been written, observes the Minister, in respect to the raising and lowering of Customs duties, and there are some impressionable minds to which *absolute free trade* and even *free ports* offer attraction; but these extreme views are impossible. The State must have revenues to promote public works, and after due study of the question the Minister decided in favour of raising the indirect taxes levied on imports and exports as a method of increasing the revenue with least prejudice to the consumer.

Turning, however, to the Report of the Collector of Customs, we find it very distinctly stated as his opinion that a falling off in the imports to the amount of $2,570,380, or 12 per cent, reduction, in 1881, compared with 1880, was mostly due to the increase in the import tariff, which was raised to cover a deficit of $1,015,428, that early declared itself in the budget or estimates for 1881.

The latest detailed report of the receipts and expenditure is that for 1881.

The total receipts were $8,612,357
„ expenditure was 8,376,419

Analysis of Revenue

Abbreviated from the Report of the Ministry of Finance

The absolute receipts for 1881 from the principal and normal sources of revenue were

Import and export duties	$4,960,603
Licenses	632,038
Stamped paper	296,797
Stamps	188,167
Direct taxes[1] on property in the capital	403,877
" " " rural departments	674,478
	$7,155,960
Duties on indirect inheritances	
Sales and rents of public lands	
Duties on seal fisheries, trade marks and patents, port dues, &c.	188,627
Amounts overdue from 1880 and collected in 1881, and various other receipts	1,267,770
	$8,612,357

Analysis of Expenditure

The expenditure for 1881 consisted of the following amounts: —

Houses of Legislature	$194,784
Department of foreign affairs	70,178
" government	660,241
" finance	543,134
" war	1,506,832
Departmental governments (*Jefaturas.*)	452,645
Public instruction	304,949
Subministrations, clothing, arms, &c.	251,012
General expenses of government	$3,983,775
Various extra expenses in the different administrations and for the public service detailed in the accounts	500,000
	$4,483,775

Service of Public Debt.

Internal debt	$1,261,800
Uruguay loan (London)	408,000
Anglo-French debt	191,140
Italian debt	74,317
Central Railway	59,570
French debt	80,064
North-West Railway, Montevideo	54,000
Redeemable debt	123,277
Redemption of paper money	180,000
Mauá Bank	204,333
	2,636,501
Sums due in 1880 and paid in 1881, and various expenses on account of the general administration and for the service of the public debt	1,256,143
	$8,376,419

Customs Duties

Comparing the Customs revenue for the year 1856 with that of 1829, there appears an increase of 145 per cent. From 1861 to 1864 an increase of 333 per cent. Comparing the year 1866 with 1869, there is an increase of 70 per cent. The Customs revenue in 1872 rose suddenly to $7,189,000, and in 1873 to $7,509,485, the highest amount it has yet attained. In 1874 it fell to $6,509,843, and in 1875 to $4,978,715. It increased in 1876, and since that date it has risen and fallen alternately until 1880, when it was reduced to $4,409,496. The fall in 1879-1880 has been ascribed to the lowering of the import duties 50 per cent, and the export duties 25 per cent. Of the beneficial effects of the low export duties, which were reduced to 6 per cent, on produce in general, there is no doubt. The import duties in 1880 on merchandise in general, but with many exceptions, were 25 per cent, on the valuation. Liquors, boots and shoes, ready-made linen, and many articles of food and general consumption in families, such as groceries, &c., pay 37 per cent. Raw materials, such as timber, iron and steel, &c., paid 15 per cent. In June, 1881, a law was passed, imposing additional duties on articles already highly taxed, to the following general effect.

An increase of 8 per cent., making 45 per cent, altogether, on spirits, manufactured tobacco, playing cards, perfumery, arms, powder and ammunition, &c.; 4 per cent, additional, or 40 per cent, altogether, on wines, boots and shoes, hats, clothing, furniture, carriages, harness, &c.; 10 per cent, additional, or 35 per cent, altogether, on unmanufactured tobacco; 5 per cent, additional, or 25 per cent., on all cotton goods and cordage; an additional export duty of 2 per cent, on wool, grease, tallow, and other articles of export included in the tariff; and ½ per cent, on dried and salted meats, &c.

In raising the duties it is thought that the Government of Uruguay was imitating the example of the United States, and pursuing a protectionist policy; but if a duty of 37 per cent, is in some senses prohibitive, and more than protectionist, it is obvious that there is no similarity in the industrial position of the Republic of Uruguay compared with that of the United States. In the former country there is no industry to speak of that needs protection, A glance at the analysis of expenditure given above, where, out of a revenue of eight millions more or less, four millions, including military requirements, are ample for the ordinary expenses of the Government, it is plain that the evil is the yearly burden of interest on debts, the accumulation of which in Uruguay, as in many larger countries, has been encouraged by the fatal facilities of indirect taxation.

In regard to the *Public Debt,* the Minister of Finance says in his report:

"Entering into other details of the administration, the most important question to notice is the conversion by a Redeemable Debt of those claims anterior to 1879, which, according to law, were in a position to be converted.

"The magnitude of that operation has entailed great labour on the department of the Accountant-General, as it involved the verification of innumerable claims extending over a number of years, and constituting what is called the 'Floating Debt.' The claims already acknowledged and converted amount to $6,473,744. Many are still pending.

"The service of the Public Debt in general — internal, funded, consolidated, external, and international — has been attended to with perfect regularity, as also the redemption of the paper money, which in April, 1882, was reduced to $2,465,000.

"Existing contracts with the holders of the internal and consolidated debts expire at the end of 1882; and at the end of January, 1883, the agreement with the holders of the Uruguay bonds in London will also expire.

"It is presumed that the creditors of the State will, for the common good, offer a reasonable basis for the new arrangements."

The Minister, at the conclusion of his report, alludes to a subject which has been a source of consolation to all who have lived or have interests in young countries; that is, "their elasticity," as it is called.

He says: — "The position of a Minister of Finance in this country, as in any other where for years past credit has been abused and the administration of its resources neglected and sacrificed to political struggles, cannot be easy; and his duties must necessarily be surrounded with difficulties that only the advantages of peace and the energy of the nation can

Description.

INTERNAL CONSOLIDATED.

Loan, Extraordinary
" Pacification, 1st series
" " 2nd "
" Extraordinary, 2nd series
Debt, Land Redemption
" Funded, 2nd series (*bis*)
" Additional [for interest], contracted 22nd October, 1875, 29th May, 1876, and 20th February, 1878
" Consolidated of 1872
" Extraordinary
" Internal, 1st series
" " 2nd "
" Central Uruguay Railway, contracted 27th November, 1877, and 25th February, 1878
" Santa Rosa Railway, by Law of 8th February, 1881
" Redeemable, by Law 9th February, 1881
" Special (for interest)
" " " corresponding to 1881
" Consolidated of 1880
  Same issued in the quarter

EXTERNAL.

Uruguay Loan, $14,715,230
Montevidean European Loan
Additional Bonds, contracted July 1st, 1878, £371,520

INTERNATIONAL.

Anglo-French Debt
Italian Debt
French Debt

---

* The redemption will be effected as soon as the line is opened.

DATED, EXTERNAL, AND INTERNATIONAL, ON 21st APRIL, 1882.

| Interest and Redemption as by agreement 20th Feb., 1878. || Amount on 31st December, 1877. | Amount on 21st April, 1882. |
Interest.	Sinking Fund.		
4 p. c.	2 p. c.	$2:931,500,00	$1:981,000,00
4 ,,	1 ,,	1:629,250,00	1:301,350,00
4 ,,	1 ,,	2:558,150,00	2:011,800,00
4 ,,	¾ ,,	4:000,000,00	3:393,500,00
4 ,,	½ ,,	1:589,807,31	1:331,254,59
4 ,,	½ ,,	1:346,000,00	1:199,000,00
4 ,,	½ ,,	3:107,022,53	3:369,794,92
3 ,,	½ ,,	2:651,308,18	2:279,027,12
2 ,,	½ ,,	2:164,111,59	1:359,023,39
2 ,,	2 ,,	739,000,00	167,500,00
2 ,,	1 ,,	4:122,734,46	2:892,055,01
4 ,,	2 ,,	..	938,000,00
4 ,, *	2 ,,	..	1:800,000,00
without interest	4 ,,	..	5:227,821,81
,, ,,	$5000 monthly.	2:739,498,24	6:162,960,15
2 p. c.	5 p. c.	..	{ 918,592,16 541,880,29
$34,000 mnthly.	..	$29:878,382,31	$37:213,559,47
..	..	14:874,560,00	14:551,200,00
..	..	..	1:746,141,00
5 p. c.	$128,000 annly.	$1:741,200,00	$1:092,000,00
5 ,,	24,000 ,,	1:101,050,00	983,850,00
4 ,,	100,000 ,, †	..	1:934,113,15
..	..	$47:595,192,31	$57:520,866,62
..	...	£10,113,978	£12,223,184

† To count from January 1st, 1884.

satisfactorily overcome. During a period of forty years of civil war *the Republic has advanced of itself,* acquiring wealth without other help than its own productive forces, its fertile soil, and superb climate...The Republic has suffered financial and economic disasters like that of 1875; but all countries have passed through similar epochs, recovering their well-being and the re-establishment of their credit by order, labour, and prudent conduct. We are now in an epoch of reconstruction. The time is gone by for insensate projects. The ruinous loans to sustain interminable civil wars can no longer be negotiated; those schemes of inconvertible and forced currencies, those violations of public credit and of the faith and honour of administrations, cannot recur. We have made too great advances in the principles of justice and equity to fall again into errors we can never sufficiently atone."

Since the date of the Minister's report a satisfactory arrangement, which came in force in January, 1883, has been concluded with the holders of the bonds of the internal, consolidated, and funded debt. Negotiations are also in progress for an arrangement with the London bondholders of the Uruguay loan.

The amount of the Public Debt, in January, 1879 — including the foreign and internal loans, the Anglo-French and Italian debts — was $47,684,940. In the Budget of 1879-80 the internal debt is placed at $30,812,701. The foreign debt at $14,551,200. The international (or Anglo-French and Italian) at $12,497,150. Total, $47,861,051.

The paper currency guaranteed by the State amounted, in 1876, to $12,125,355. In the years 1876, 1877, and 1878, a sum amounting to $7,850,259 was redeemed. In January, 1879, there remained for redemption — or amortization, which is continued regularly month by month — $4,275,077, and, as stated above, in 1881-82 the amount was further reduced to $2,465,000.

At the end of the year 1881 the total amount of the Public Debt of the Republic of Uruguay was $57,834,611. The accounts, however, are published in the Minister's report up to April 21, 1882, when, after the redemptions effected in the three months previously, the total debt stood at $57,520,866, or 12,223,184*l.* sterling.

The preceding is a condensed epitome of the details given in the tables contained in that report. It has not been thought necessary to show here the yearly redemptions, but only the total amount of the debt in 1877 before certain agreements were made with the creditors in the following year, and the amount of the debt as it stood in 1882, after the redemptions made in the interval, and with the additional obligations contracted since 1877.

In the present year 1883, schemes have been set on foot, and are being actively pursued, for the establishment of a National Bank; the construction of Harbour Works at Montevideo, and also for the unification of the whole debt of the Republic.

Meanwhile, the public revenue increases. In the Budget for 1883, the estimates are.

At the end of 1870 the issue of the private banks was	$3,352,000
Issue guaranteed by the State	7,357,365
	$10,609,365

Of the estimated amount of Receipts for 1883, $6,000,000 are derived from Custom dues.

[1] By a law passed in 1882 the rate of the property tax or *contribucion directa* is 5½ per cent, in the departments and 5 per cent, in the capital. On gardens and farm lands the rate is 4} in the departments and 4 per cent in the metropolitan department. The collectors of the tax received 4 per cent, on the amount recovered, but by a recent law this payment of the collectors by commission has been abolished.

Public Works and Institutions

Montevideo, the most important banks of issue, discount, and deposit, &c., are the London and River Plate Bank and the Banco Comercial. After these come the London and Brazilian Bank — not a bank of issue; the Bank of Villaamil and Co., with an issue reduced to $10,430; [1] the Mercantile Bank of the River Plate, and some other establishments, which, without bearing the title of banks, receive deposits and deal in loans, discounts, and bill operations.

All the banks are subject to legislative restrictions, principally in regard to the issue of notes, which is guaranteed by metallic reserves to the extent of one-third of the issue. In other respects the banks are jointstock or private institutions.

In 1867 the paper issue of the country amounted to $7,160,374. In the month and year of the great crisis, November, 1868, it amounted to $11,097,017.

At the end of 1870 the issue of the private banks was	$3,352,000
Issue guaranteed by the State	7,357,365
	$10,609,365

At the commencement of 1873 the paper in circulation was —

Private banks	$6,544,042
Guaranteed by the State	3,512,164
	$10,056,164

In 1872 and 1873 the money obtained by the Uruguay loan in London was applied to the payment of the English debt, to the redemption of the notes of the *Platense, Montevideano* and others, and to the payment or conversion in gold of the bank notes which the nation had guaranteed. In two years the State converted $5,961,861 of paper.

In prosperous times the Republic, to extend its internal transactions, is supposed to require a note circulation of at least ten millions of dollars. At present the note circulation is not one-third of that amount.

"Credit establishments in the Republic are few," says the Minister of Finance in his report of 1882, "and above all their capital and functions are limited. The London and River Plate Bank and the Commercial Bank deserve the complete confidence they have been enabled to sustain and justify in all epochs by prudent and proper management. But the capital they employ is not very large, and their operations are confined to Montevideo; whereas in the rural districts the notes of the banks, notwithstanding their credit, do not circulate for want of affiliated institutions or agencies to cash their notes and extend their operations.

"It is precisely in the rural districts, where the true wealth of the country exists, that the credit establishments should facilitate operations, for their own profit as well as that of the country.

"In Salto, Paysandú, Cerro Largo, Tacuarembó, Canelones, &c., departments of the first importance, possessing a commerce and industry to be valued by millions, there is not a single bank to aid their development.

"The banks actually in existence are useful to the trade of the city of Montevideo, inasmuch as they discount the trade bills and promissory notes, but their benefits do not reach the rural and agricultural classes, or even the small traders of the towns of the interior; and for the reason already adduced, that neither the amount of their capital, nor their regulations, are adapted to thus extend operations. This is all the more to be regretted in view of the increasing prosperity of the Republic." [2]

The first dry dock constructed in the Port of Montevideo was the Maua dock, which has proved of great service in the repairs of vessels of average tonnage. Subsequently another of greater dimensions, and capable of holding the largest vessels frequenting the River Plate, was constructed by Messrs. Jackson and Cibils. It is divided into two departments, one serving as a dry dock, and the other as a floating dock, for the loading and discharge of vessels. The two departments are separated by dock-gates supported by granite piers, and the whole work is solid, and a credit to the port and to the founders. The length of the dock is 137 mètres, the two divisions being respectively 59 mètres and 77 mètres long. The width of the dock is 17 mètres at the level of the quays, and 12 mètres below. At low tide there is about 16 feet of water, and at high tide about

19. The entrance is easy, and protected from the south-west winds by a natural reef as well as by a well-constructed breakwater.

For the last twelve years, since 1871, the City of Montevideo has been abundantly supplied with water of remarkable purity, compared with the supplies of several large cities in Great Britain. The works are situated on the River Santa Lucía, near a village of the same name, about 33 miles from Montevideo. They are due to private enterprise, and were until lately the property of Messrs. Lezica, Lanuz, & Fynn, by whom they were initiated. They are now the property of a London company. The works were planned and constructed by the English engineer, Mr. Frederick Newman. The reservoir is placed at the distance of about two miles from Las Piedras, a village near Montevideo, and holds upwards of 30,000 pipes, or 3,000,000 gallons of water. The elevation of the reservoir is 160 feet above the level of one of the central squares of the city. According to the analysis made by Messrs. Parodi & Isola, the waters of the Santa Lucia run over a bed of primitive rock of granite, gneiss, and feldspar, &c., which accounts for the small proportion they contain of mineral and organic substances. Compared with the water supplied to four large cities in Great Britain, the analysis of the supply at Montevideo is classified as follows: —

	Solid.	Grains per Gallon. Organic.	Grains per Gallon. Total.	Hardness.
Birmingham	37·70	1·65	39·35	15·5
Liverpool	14·64	0·55	15·19	9·6
Glasgow	1·90	0·30	2·20	1·0
Manchester	4·17	0·25	4·42	2·5
Montevideo	4·62	0·70	5·32	2·0

The Montevideo waterworks were commenced in April, 1870, and were inaugurated on the 18th July, 1871. It speaks something for the beauty of "The Camp" — or undulating grass-lands of the Banda Oriental — that upwards of 20,000 tons of iron piping, employed in the construction of the works, were easily conveyed in bullock-carts from Montevideo to the banks of the Santa Lucia, without other road or pathway than nature had provided in the solid but elastic turf.

The River Plate Telegraph Company (Limited) was inaugurated in 1872. The wires extend over most Departments of the Republic, and a submarine cable belonging to the company unites Montevideo with Buenos Aires, whence a land line extends through the Argentine Republic to Chile.

The Platino-Brazilian Telegraph Company's land line commenced in 1872, and there is a cable from Montevideo to Brazil belonging to the Western and Brazilian Telegraph Company.

The railways in operation are the Central Uruguay, from Montevideo to Las Piedras, Canelones, Santa Lucia, Florida, and Durazno, with a branch to San José, and an extension in construction to Higueritas. The Northern Railway, that commenced to work in 1877, from Montevideo to the Barra of Santa Lucia, in connection with a tramway of the same name, which encircles the City. The Salto and Santa Rosa Railway, not yet concluded. The first section only is open.

The Central Uruguay Railway, as far as it is at present completed, extends from Montevideo to the north bank of the River Yi, just beyond Durazno, about 130 miles in all. It is in contemplation to establish a system of carriage by carts, in connection with the line between the Yi terminus and the districts of Cerro Largo and Tacuarembó, and to book goods from those districts to Montevideo and *vice versa*.

The Higueritas extension is completed only as far as San José. Another proposed extension northwards, as far as Santa Ana, on the Brazilian frontier [see map], will be of immense benefit to the Central Railway as well as to the country in general; and its completion will probably be one of the first results of a hoped-for period of peace and prosperity.

"The Central Uruguay Railway," says the Report of the Ministry of Finance (1882) "possesses a great future to the benefit both of the country and the shareholders. Some idea of its importance may be gathered from the following results in the years 1880, 1881, and the first three months of the year 1882.

The Bonds were quoted in London thus: —

		£		
In 1880	..	Capital 470,000	..	3 per cent premium
,, 1881	..	,, 470,000	..	14 ,, ,,
,, 1882	..	,, 510,000	..	22 ,, ,,

Showing an increase of premium of 19 per cent, in less than two years. The ordinary shares, not fully paid up, were worth —

		£		£ s.
In 1880	..	Capital 94,562 shares, 10 each	..	7 10
,, 1881	..	,, 100,000 ,, 10 ,,	..	8 0
,, 1882	..	,, 100,000 ,, 10 ,,	..	9 2

"The value of the property is assured not only by the excellence of its directorate and administration, but also by the wealth and progress of the country favouring its future extension, so as to increase its value. It is absolutely indispensable that the shareholders in England should understand that the line cannot remain stationary at Durazno. It must, in short, pass the Rio Negro, so as to embrace the superior richness of the Northern Departments and the commerce and industries which arise in those districts and find an outlet in the ports of the River Uruguay.

"The net profits of the line in 1881 were 23½ dollars per cent, more than in 1880. The goods traffic increased in the same period 21½ dollars per cent. The gross weight of the goods carried showed an increase of more than 34 2/3 tons per cent.

The Pando Railway, which is now open as far as that place, will be eventually extended to Minas, one of the centres of the mineral and mining districts.

There is almost daily communication by the river steamers with Buenos Aires and the ports of Uruguay; and at the present time few hours pass without the arrival of a seagoing or ocean-steamer from the ports of Brazil or Europe.

The English lines of steamers to Montevideo are those of the Royal Mail Company, from Southampton; the Liverpool, Brazil, and River Plate Company, and the Pacific Steam Navigation Company, from Liverpool.

Fares:— 25*l*. & 35*l*. first class; 20*l*. & 25*l*. second class; 12*l*. third class.

The trip from Liverpool or Southampton or Montevideo — with a few hours' stoppage at Lisbon, St. Vincent, Pernambuco, Bahia, and Rio Janeiro; or by a more direct route, with fewer calling places— occupies from 23 to 30 days, and, generally speaking — and particularly in the months of March, April, and May, and September and October, when there is more chance of fine weather on both sides of the line — it is, without exception, the most enjoyable of all ocean voyages.

The offices of the Royal Mail Company are at 18, Moorgate-street, London.

The offices of the London, Brazil, and River Plate Company, Water street, Liverpool; 17, Leadenhall-street, London.

The offices of the Pacific Steam Navigation Company, 5 & 7, Fenchurch-street, London; 31, James street, Liverpool; 22, Royal Exchange-square, Glasgow.

There are eight lines of Tramways intersecting the City, and extending to the suburban resorts known as Reducto, Union, Paso Molino, the Cerro, &c.

The River Plate Telephone Company is working at Montevideo; and telephonic communication is becoming customary.

Money, Weights and Measures

The standard currency in Uruguay is gold. The nominal unit is the gold doubloon, value 10 dollars silver. The doubloon, however, is not yet coined. The silver coins are the dollar, and pieces of 50, 20, and 10 cents each. 4.70 dollars = 1*l*. 1 dollar = 4*s*. 3*d*.

The Metrical System of weights and measures has been officially adopted since 1862, but the old measures are still in use.

```
100 lbs. Spanish = quintal ............ 101·40 lbs. avoirdupois.
  1 arrobe ..................................... 25 lbs.
  4 arrobes .................................... 1 quintal.
 20 quintals, 80 arrobes, or 2000 lbs. ........ 1 ton.
225 lbs. = 1 fanega (chiefly used as a measure for grain, and in
    some cases the fanega varies).
  1 vara (Spanish yard) 2 feet 10 inches, or 859 lineal mètre.
  1 cuadra, or "square" ............... 100 varas in length.
 60 cuadras ......................... 1 league in length.
3600 square cuadras.. ................ 1 square league.
  1 square league, 6564 acres, or 10⅗ths English square miles.
  1 mètre ............................ 1196 square yards
  1 hectare (10 mètres)    32,809 English feet, or 2·47 English
    acres.
  1 cuadra ........................... 1-82 English acres.
```

Large pieces of land are purchased by the square league, or by the *suerte* of 2700 square *cuadras,* equal to one league and a half in length by half a league in width, or three quarters of a square league — or 4923 square acres, 333 square yards.

In Buenos Aires the *cuadra* is 150 varas long, or 40 cuadras the league; or 16000.9 cuadras to the square league. A square *cuadra* — or *manzana* — in Buenos Aires covers a fraction more than 4 English acres.

[1] The Bank of Villaamil and Co. has, since this was written, been placed in liquidation.
[2] The scarcity of banking accommodation noticed by the Minister has already attracted attention. A scheme for the formation of a National Bank is referred to, page 155.

Lightning Source UK Ltd.
Milton Keynes UK
UKHW011525141022
410475UK00001B/50